BATMAN
BLOODSTORM

DC Comics

DC Comics

Jenette Kahn, President & Editor-in-Chief

Paul Levitz, Executive Vice President & Publisher

Dennis O'Neil, Group Editor

Jordan B. Gorfinkel, Assistant Editor

Georg Brewer, Design Director

Robbin Brosterman, Senior Art Director

Richard Bruning, VP-Creative Director

Patrick Caldon, Senior VP-Finance & Operations

Dorothy Crouch, VP-Licensed Publishing

Terri Cunningham, VP-Managing Editor

Joel Ehrlich, Senior VP-Advertising & Promotions

Alison Gill, Executive Director-Manufacturing

Lillian Laserson, VP & General Counsel

Jim Lee, Editorial Director-WildStorm

John Nee, VP & General Manager-WildStorm

Cheryl Rubin, VP-Licensing & Merchandising

Bob Wayne, VP-Sales & Marketing

DC Comics, 1700 Broadway,
New York, NY 10019
A division of Warner Bros. -
An AOL Time Warner Company
Printed in Canada. Third Printing.
ISBN: 1-56389-185-9

Cover illustration by Kelley Jones.
Cover color by Les Dorscheid.

BATMAN
BLOODSTORM

writer DOUG MOENCH *penciller* KELLEY JONES

inker JOHN BEATTY

colorist LES DORSCHEID *letterer* TODD KLEIN

BATMAN *created by* BOB KANE

*F*or Debra, my favorite preacher of the night— DM

*F*or Peter Cushing and all his fans— KJ

*F*or Christie— JB

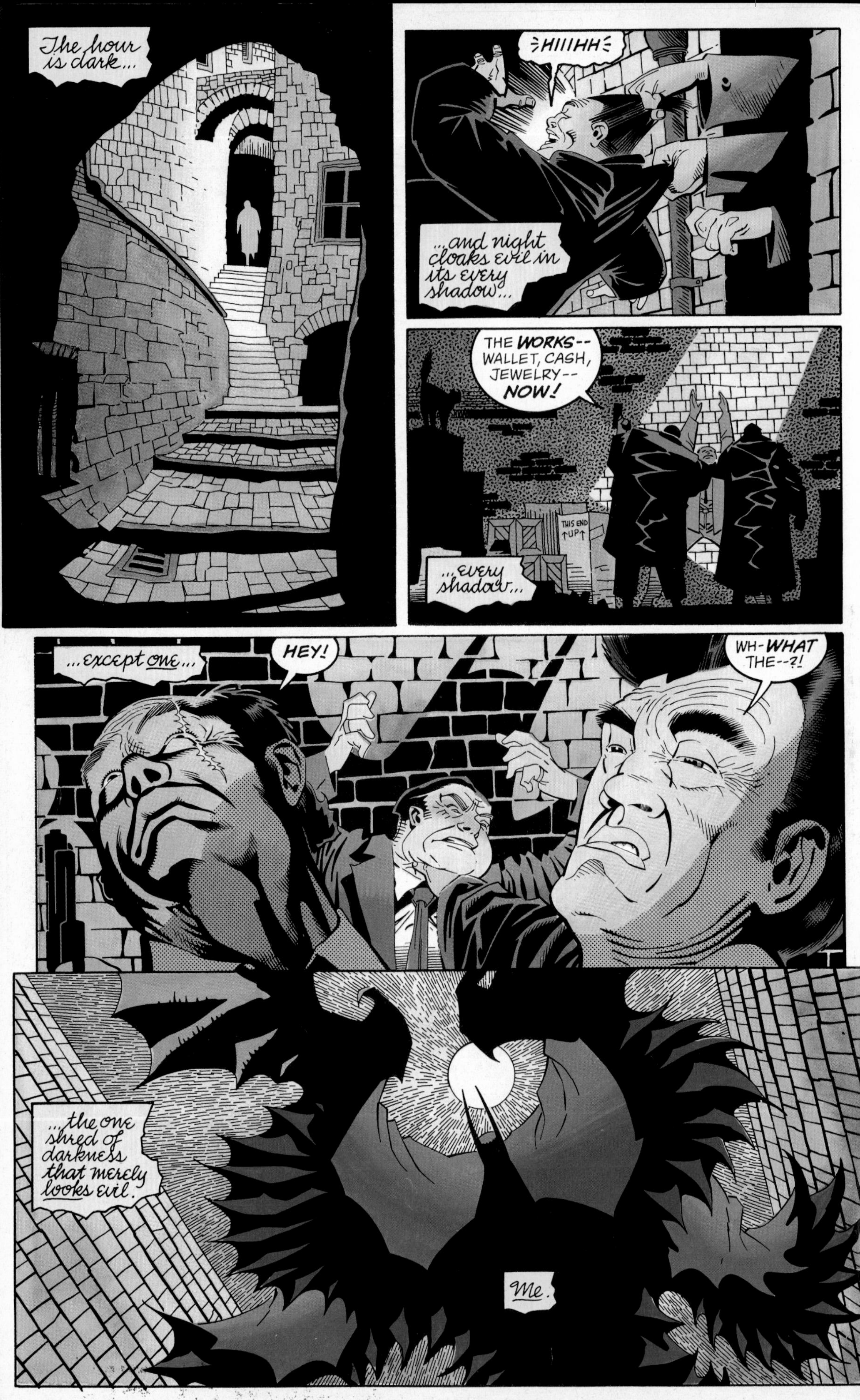

The hour is dark...
HIIIHH
...and night cloaks evil in its every shadow...
THE WORKS--WALLET, CASH, JEWELRY--NOW!
THIS END UP
...every shadow...
...except one...
HEY!
WH-WHAT THE--?!
...the one shred of darkness that merely looks evil.
Me.

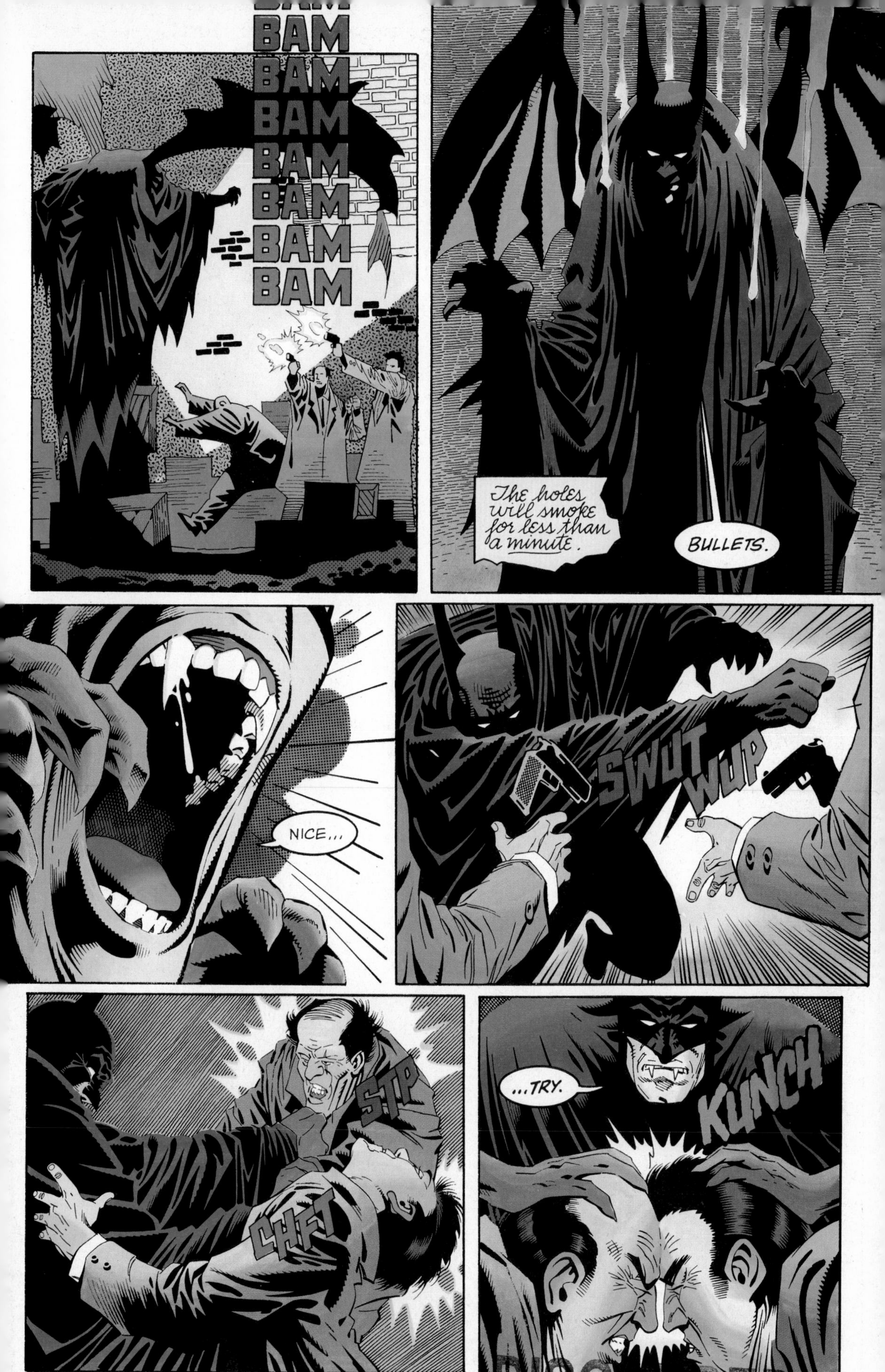
BAM
BAM
BAM
BAM
BAM
BAM
BAM
The holes will smoke for less than a minute.
BULLETS.
NICE...
SWUT
WUP
STP
CHFT
...TRY.
KUNCH

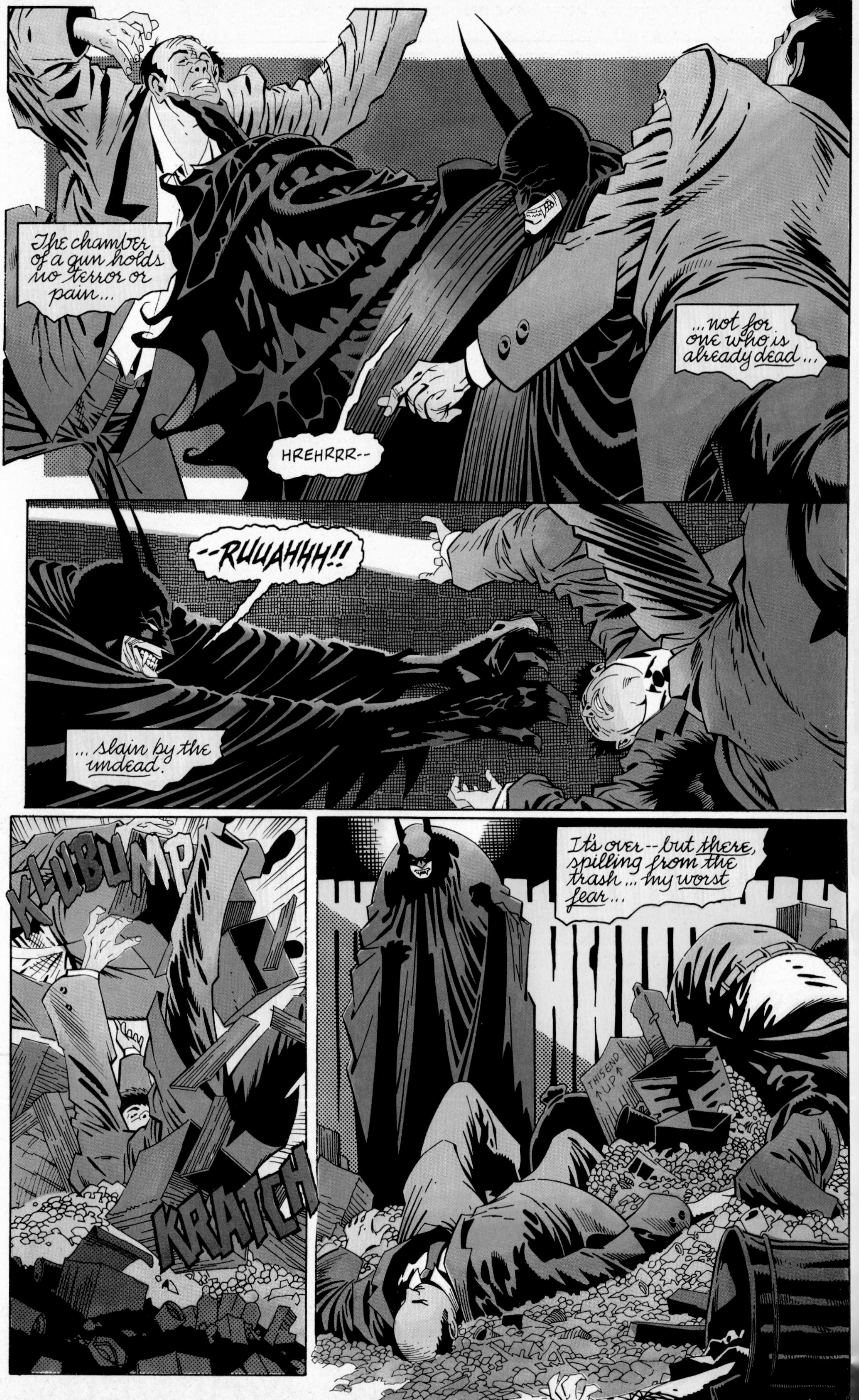
The chamber of a gun holds no terror or pain...
...not for one who is already dead...
HREHRRR--
--RUUAHHH!!
...slain by the undead.
KLUBUMP
KRATCH
It's over--but there, spilling from the trash... my worst fear...
THIS END UP

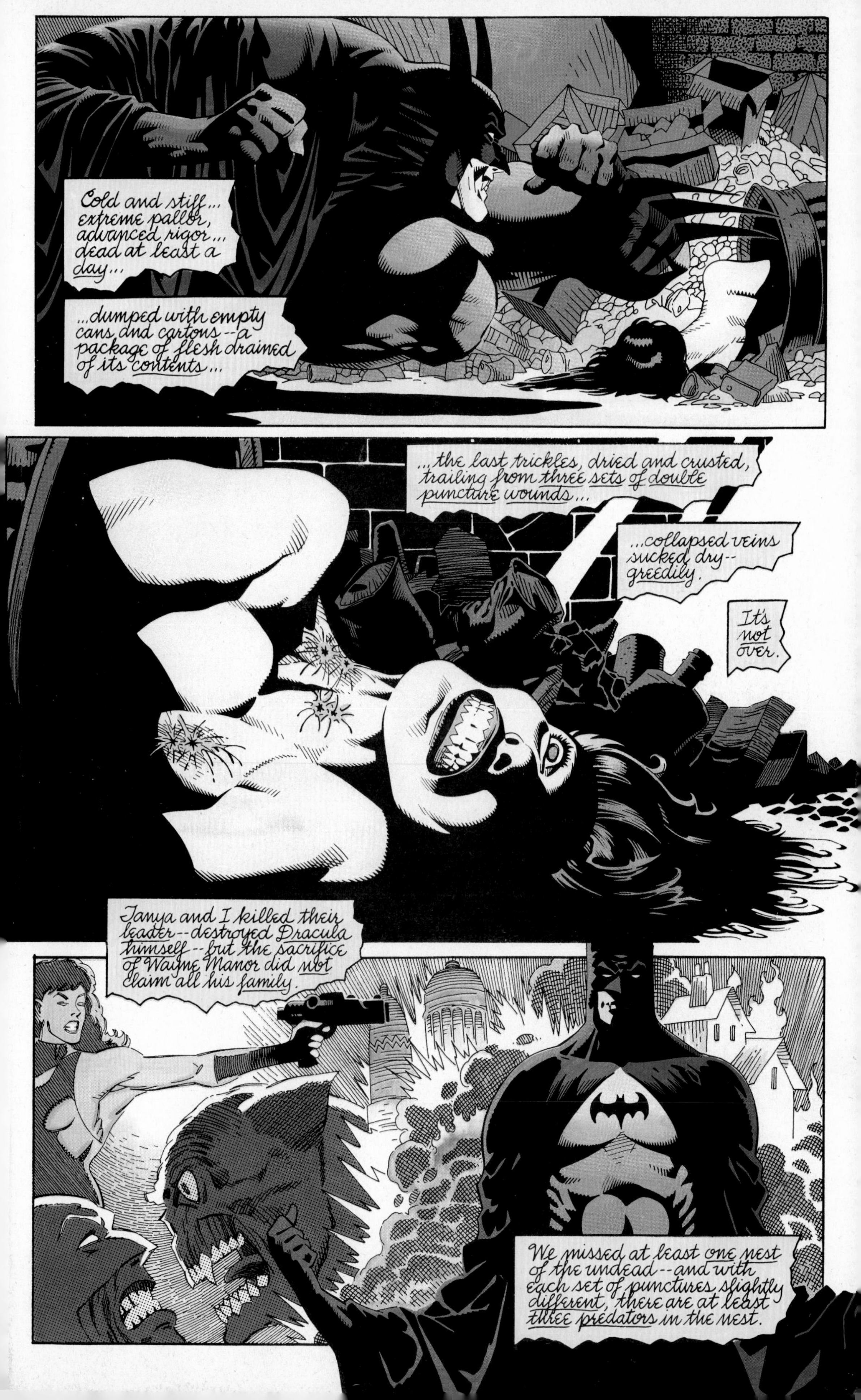
Cold and stiff... extreme pallor, advanced rigor... dead at least a day...
...dumped with empty cans and cartons--a package of flesh drained of its contents...
...the last trickles, dried and crusted, trailing from three sets of double puncture wounds...
...collapsed veins sucked dry--greedily.
It's not over.
Tanya and I killed their leader--destroyed Dracula himself--but the sacrifice of Wayne Manor did not claim all his family.
We missed at least one nest of the undead--and with each set of punctures slightly different, there are at least three predators in the nest.

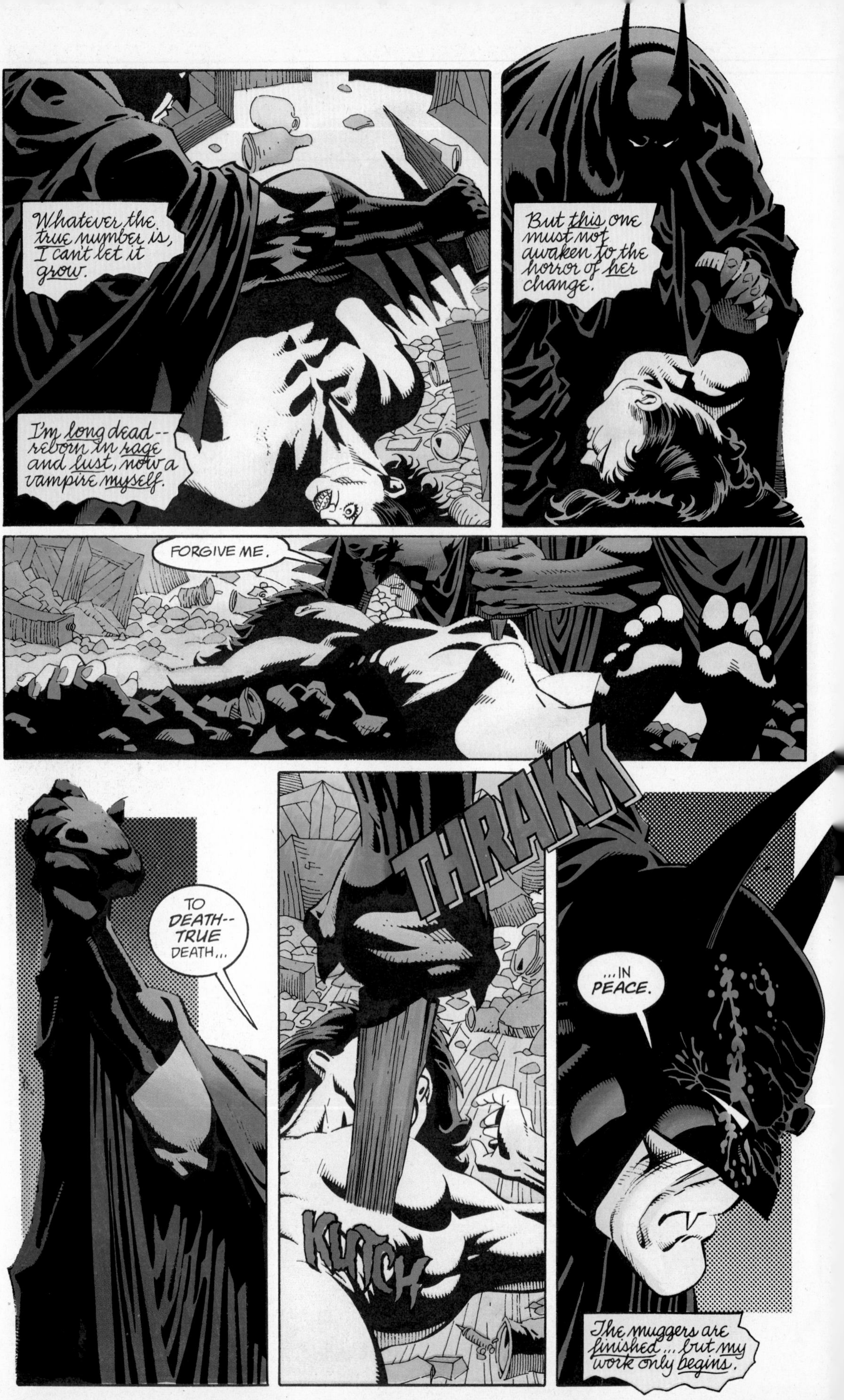

Whatever the true number is, I can't let it grow.
I'm long dead-- reborn in rage and lust, now a vampire myself.
But this one must not awaken to the horror of her change.
FORGIVE ME.
TO DEATH-- TRUE DEATH...
THRAKK
KLITCH
...IN PEACE.
The muggers are finished... but my work only begins.

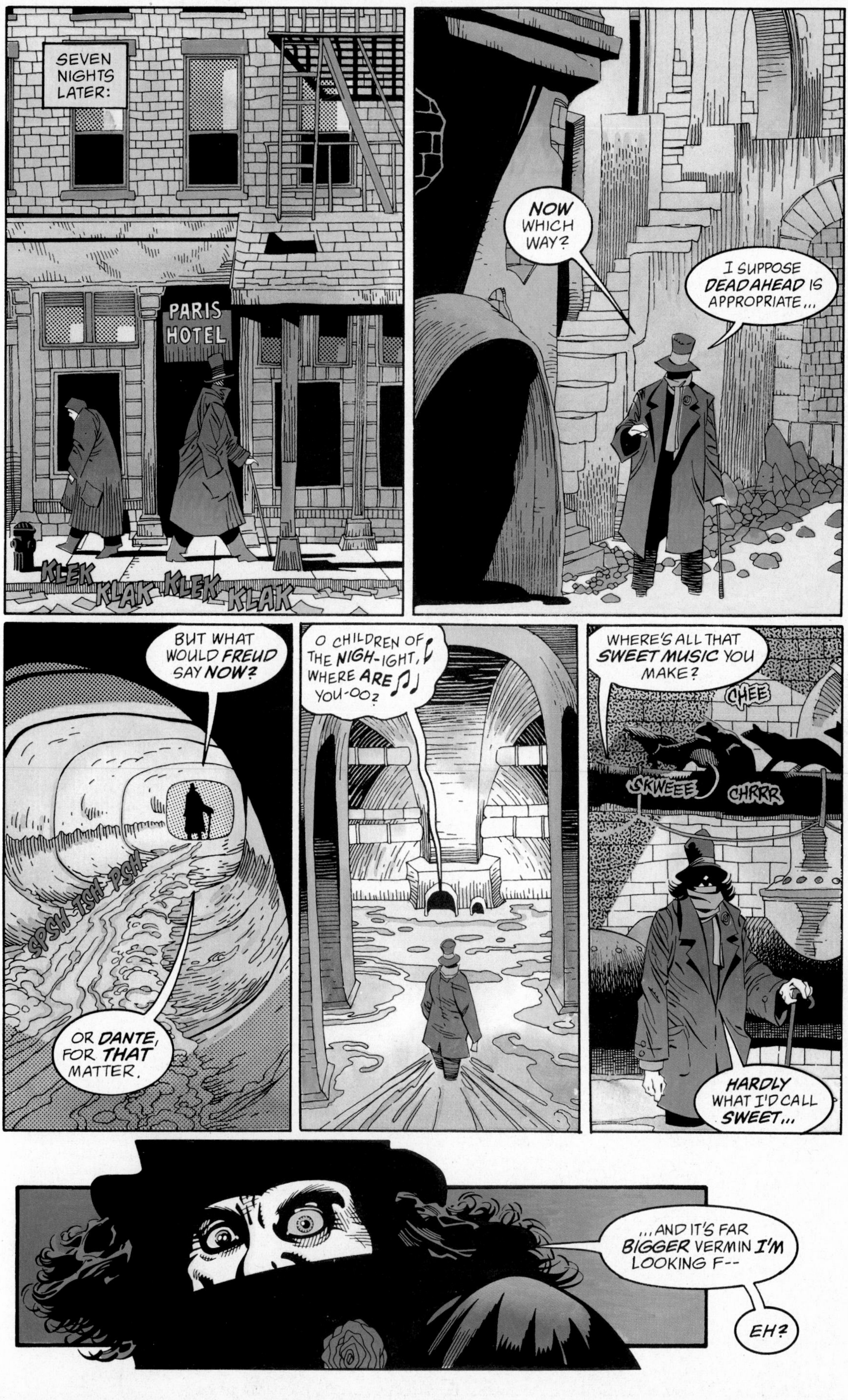

SEVEN NIGHTS LATER:
PARIS HOTEL
KLEK KLAK KLEK KLAK
NOW WHICH WAY?
I SUPPOSE DEAD AHEAD IS APPROPRIATE...
BUT WHAT WOULD FREUD SAY NOW?
SPSH TSH PSH
OR DANTE, FOR THAT MATTER.
O CHILDREN OF THE NIGH-IGHT, WHERE ARE YOU-OO?
WHERE'S ALL THAT SWEET MUSIC YOU MAKE?
CHEE
SKWEEE
CHRRR
HARDLY WHAT I'D CALL SWEET...
...AND IT'S FAR BIGGER VERMIN I'M LOOKING F--
EH?

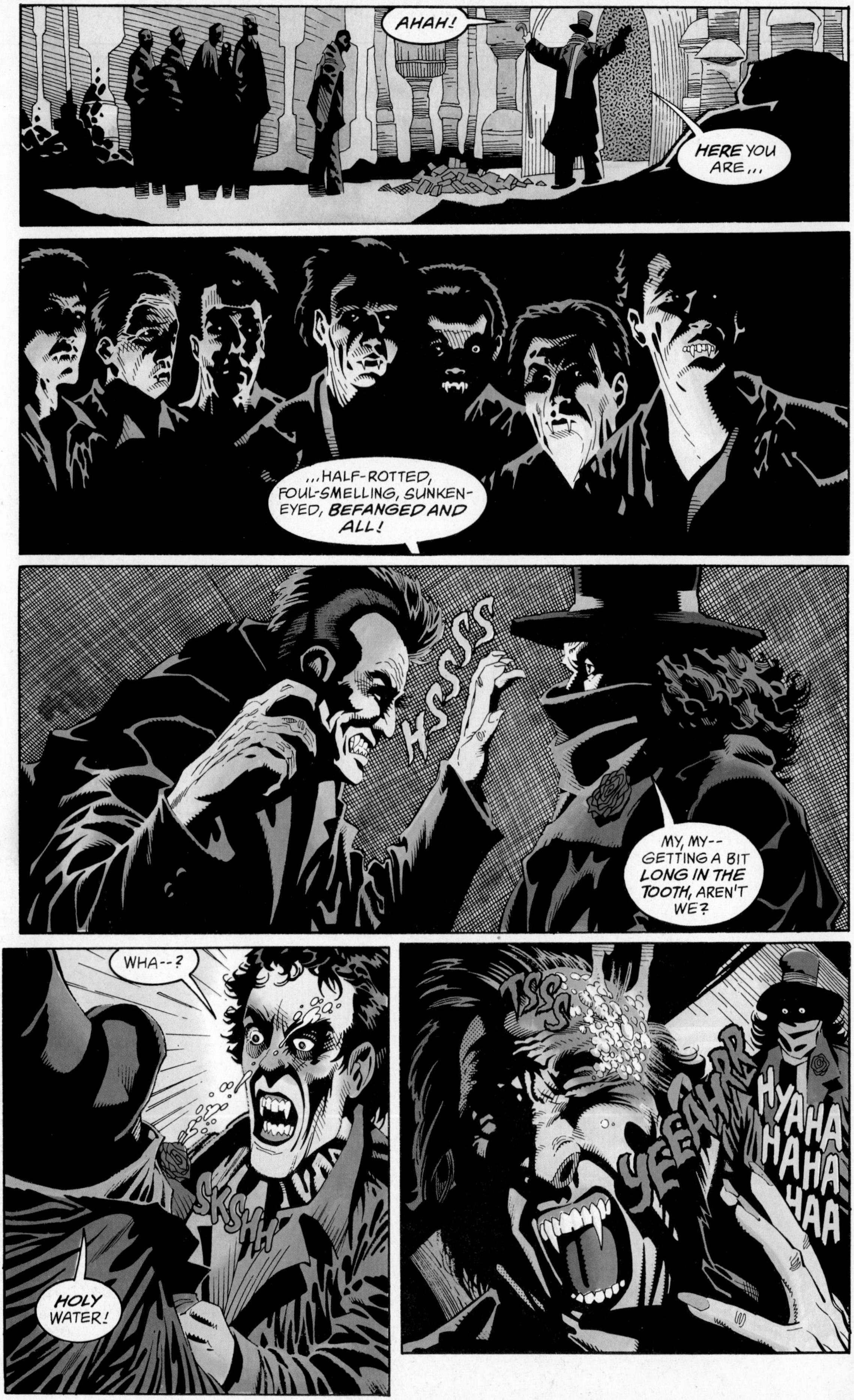
AHAH!
HERE YOU ARE,..
..,HALF-ROTTED, FOUL-SMELLING, SUNKEN-EYED, BEFANGED AND ALL!
HSSSS
MY, MY--GETTING A BIT LONG IN THE TOOTH, AREN'T WE?
WHA--?
SKSHH
HOLY WATER!
TSSS
YEEAHRR
HYAHA HAHA HAHA HAA

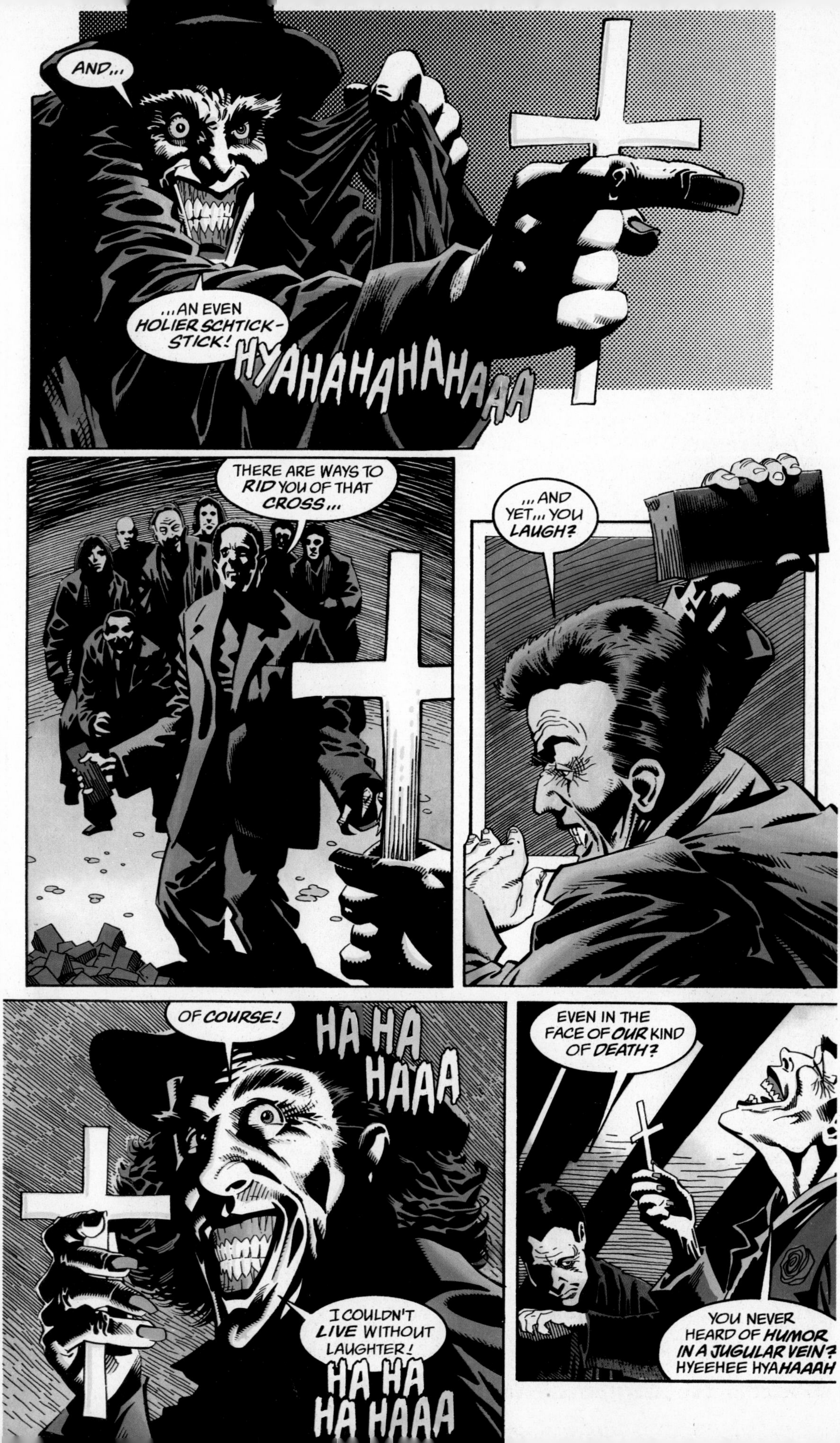
AND...
...AN EVEN HOLIER SCHTICK-STICK!
HYAHAHAHAHAHAAA
THERE ARE WAYS TO RID YOU OF THAT CROSS...
...AND YET... YOU LAUGH?
OF COURSE!
HA HA HAAA
I COULDN'T LIVE WITHOUT LAUGHTER!
HA HA HA HAAA
EVEN IN THE FACE OF OUR KIND OF DEATH?
YOU NEVER HEARD OF HUMOR IN A JUGULAR VEIN? HYEEHEE HYAHAAAH

BUT... WHY?

BECAUSE WHAT YOU'RE CONTEMPLATING IS *RIDICULOUS* -- THE PINNACLE OF INANE, SHORTSIGHTED *ABSURDITY!*

HA HA HA HAAA

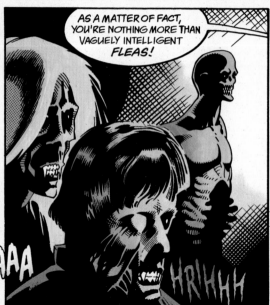

AS A MATTER OF FACT, YOU'RE NOTHING MORE THAN VAGUELY INTELLIGENT *FLEAS!*

HRIHHH

ANTHROPOMORPHIC *LEECHES!* MOSQUITOES WALKING *ERECT!* STUPID BLOODSUCKERS WITHOUT A CAUSE! YOU'VE LOST YOUR *LEADER* AND NOW YOU CAN'T THINK PAST YOUR OWN GREEDY *FANGS!*

WHAT ARE YOU--

SURE, YOU *COULD* DO THE OBVIOUS THING AND SLURP MY COLD, THIN *BLOOD*...

YOU *COULD* TURN ME INTO EXACTLY WHAT *YOU* ARE -- ANOTHER MINDLESS SLAVE TO *BLOODLUST* -- FUNCTIONING LIKE AN *ANIMAL* AND ONLY IN *DARKNESS*...

...COMPLETELY *HELPLESS* AND *VULNERABLE* DURING THE *DAY*...

OR... YOU COULD *FOREGO* MY BLOOD -- AND IT'S NOT GOOD, TRUST ME, I'VE *TASTED* IT -- AND *EMBRACE* ME FOR WHAT I AM...

...YOUR *NEW* LEADER!

HEH HEH HEEE

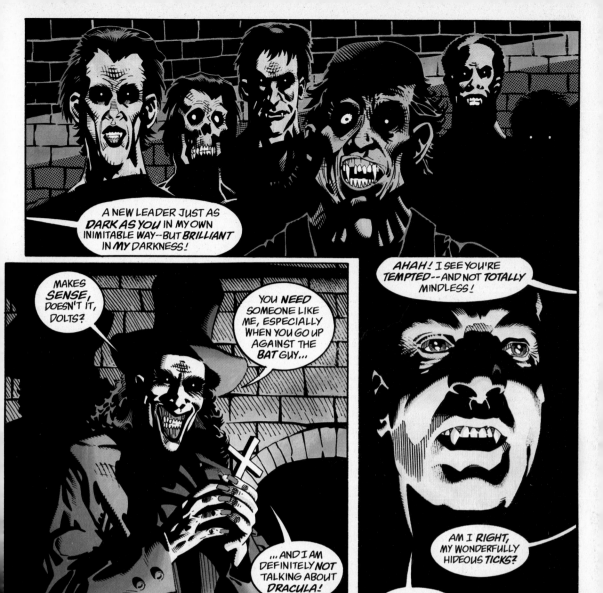

A NEW LEADER JUST AS *DARK AS YOU* IN MY OWN INIMITABLE WAY--BUT *BRILLIANT* IN *MY DARKNESS!*

MAKES *SENSE,* DOESN'T IT, DOLTS?

YOU *NEED* SOMEONE LIKE ME, ESPECIALLY WHEN YOU GO UP AGAINST THE *BAT GUY...*

...AND I AM DEFINITELY *NOT* TALKING ABOUT *DRACULA!*

AHAH! I SEE YOU'RE *TEMPTED*--AND NOT *TOTALLY* MINDLESS!

AM I *RIGHT,* MY *WONDERFULLY* HIDEOUS *TICKS?*

THE *NAME...* IS... *CREACH!*

THEN *ADMIT* IT, MISTER CREACH!

YOU *KNOW* I CAN BLAZE YOUR LURID *TRAIL OF BLOOD!*

BESIDES, I'M THE *ONLY* ONE IN *GOTHAM*--

--WITH *BETTER TEETH* THAN YOU!

NYURHUR HUR HUR HEEEE

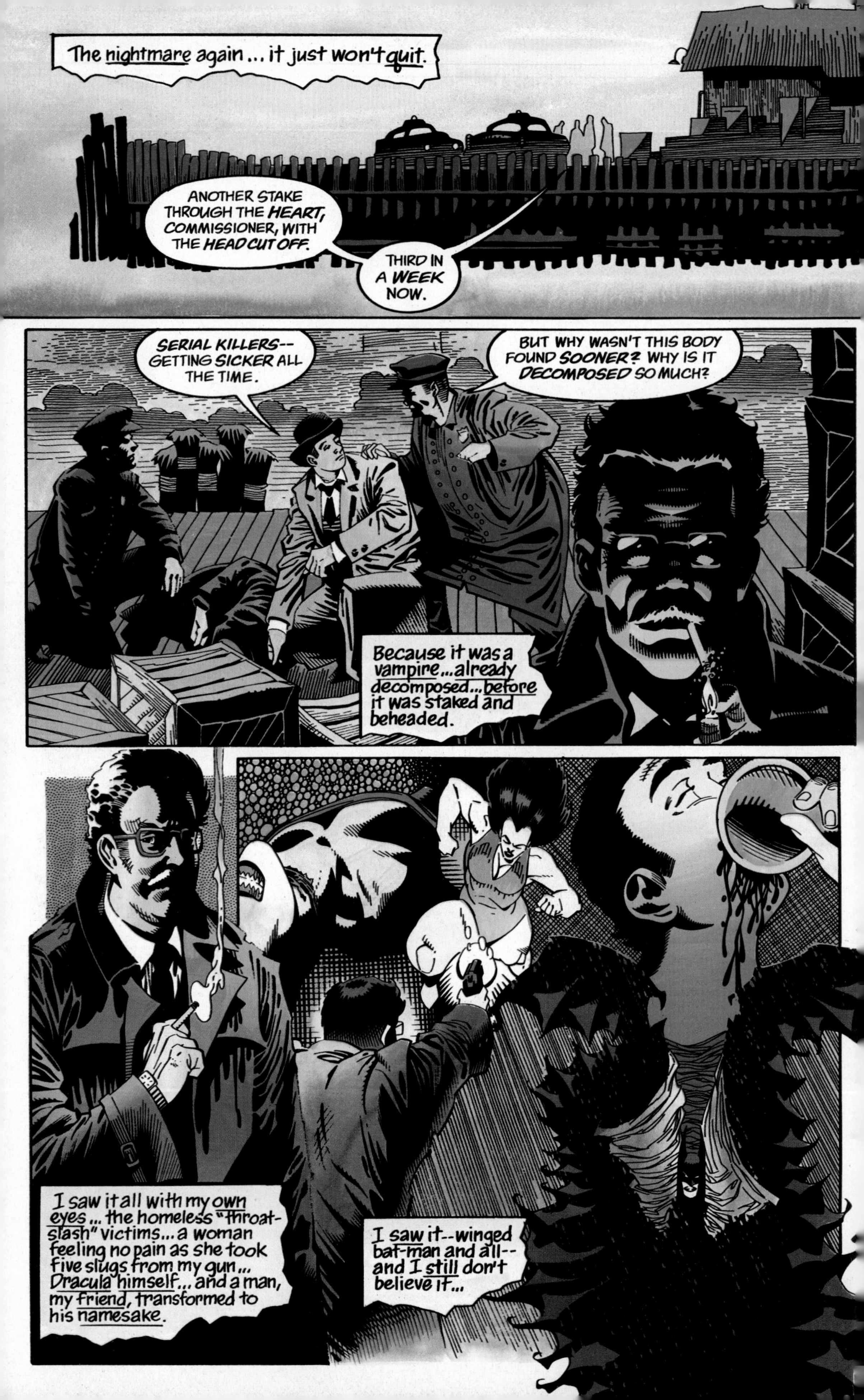
The nightmare again ... it just won't quit.
ANOTHER STAKE THROUGH THE HEART, COMMISSIONER, WITH THE HEAD CUT OFF.
THIRD IN A WEEK NOW.
SERIAL KILLERS-- GETTING SICKER ALL THE TIME.
BUT WHY WASN'T THIS BODY FOUND SOONER? WHY IS IT DECOMPOSED SO MUCH?
Because it was a vampire...already decomposed...before it was staked and beheaded.
I saw it all with my own eyes ... the homeless "throat-slash" victims... a woman feeling no pain as she took five slugs from my gun... Dracula himself... and a man, my friend, transformed to his namesake.
I saw it--winged bat-man and all-- and I still don't believe it...

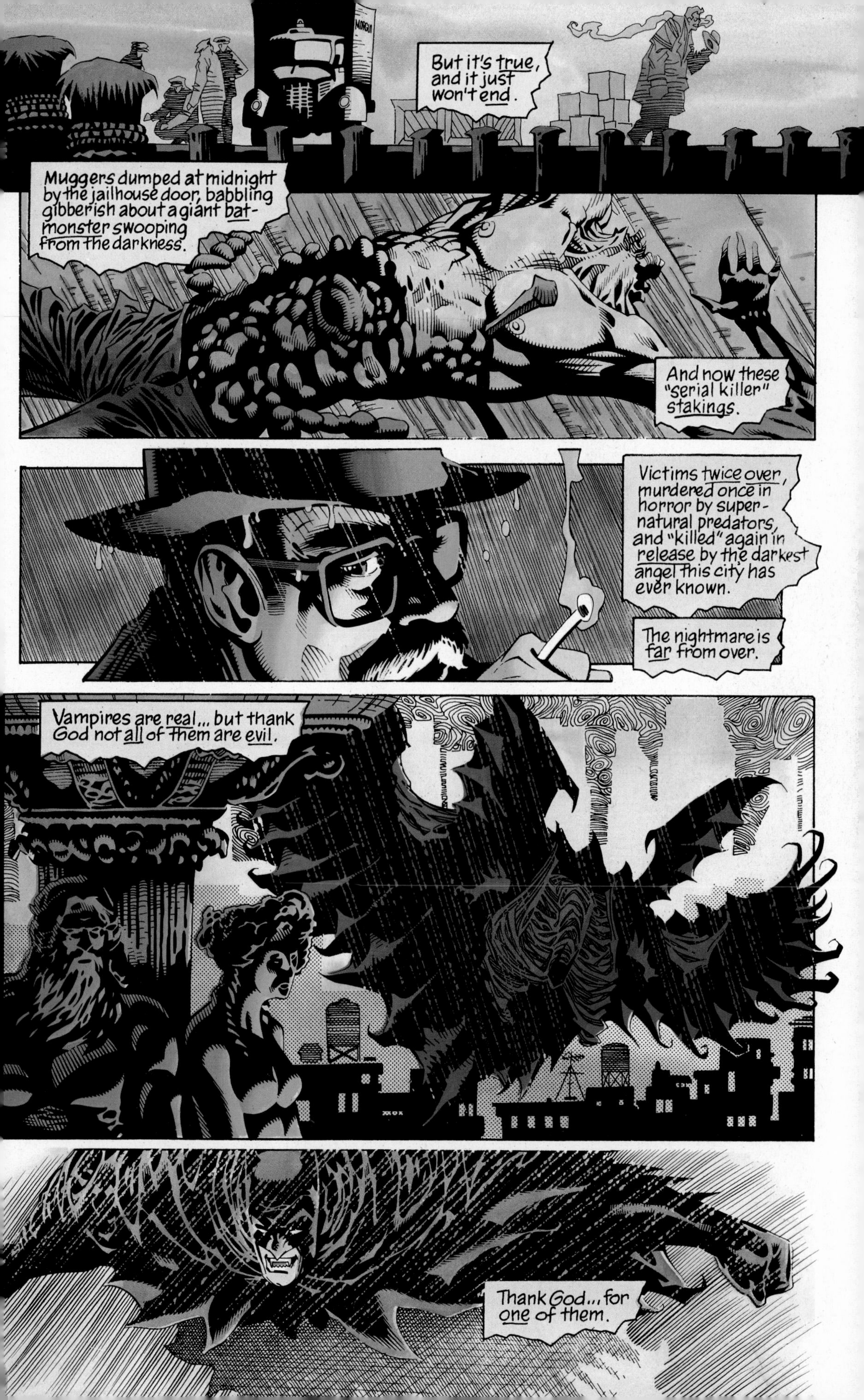
But it's true, and it just won't end.
Muggers dumped at midnight by the jailhouse door, babbling gibberish about a giant bat-monster swooping from the darkness.
And now these "serial killer" stakings.
Victims twice over, murdered once in horror by super-natural predators, and "killed" again in release by the darkest angel this city has ever known.
The nightmare is far from over.
Vampires are real... but thank God not all of them are evil.
Thank God... for one of them.

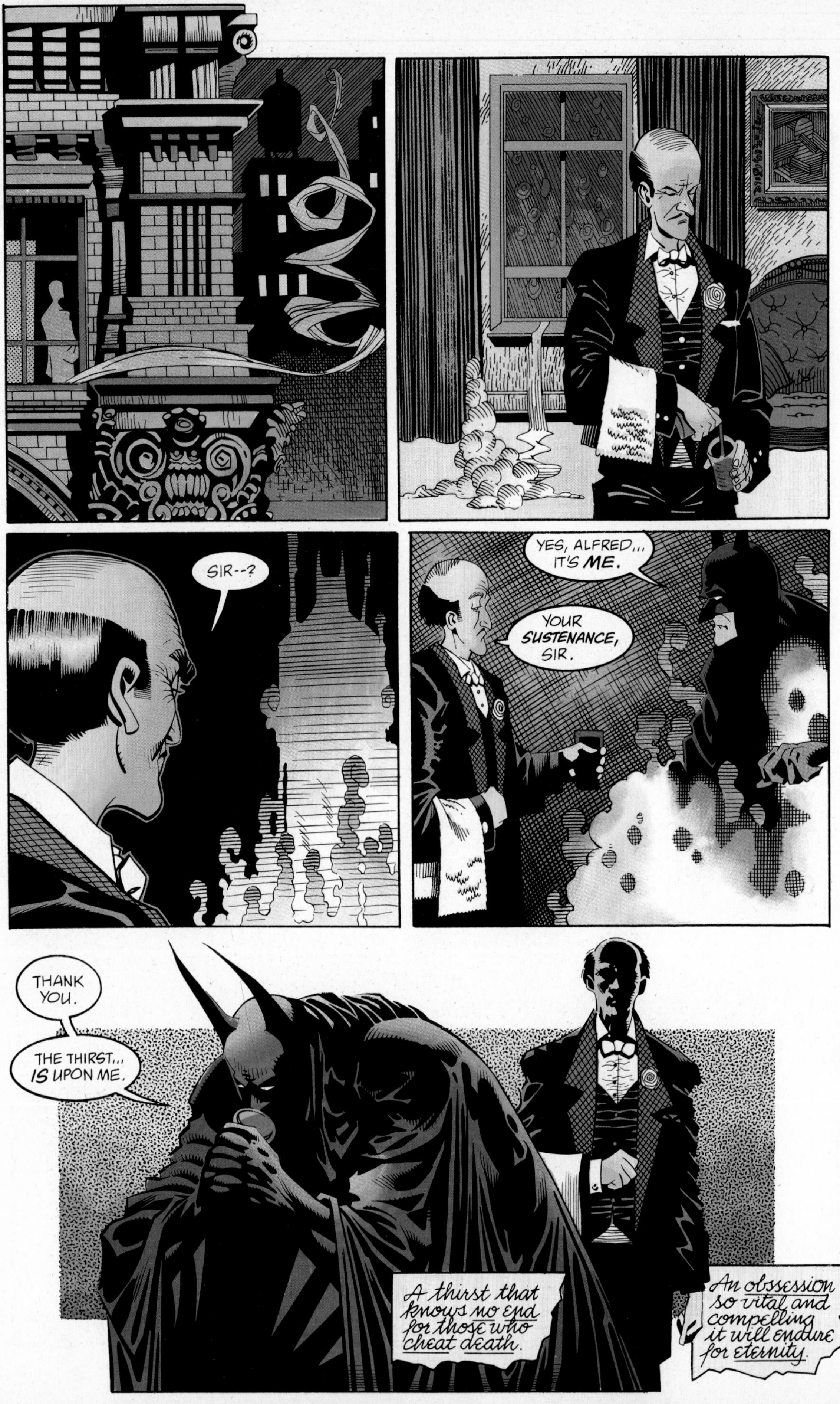
SIR--?
YES, ALFRED... IT'S ME.
YOUR SUSTENANCE, SIR.
THANK YOU.
THE THIRST... IS UPON ME.
A thirst that knows no end for those who cheat death.
An obssession so vital and compelling it will endure for eternity.

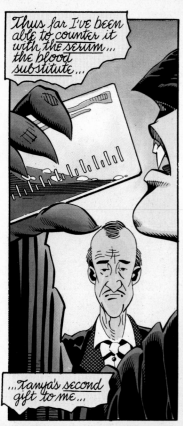

Thus far I've been able to counter it... the blood substitute...

...Tanya's second gift to me...

...made necessary by her first and more personal gift...the gift of vampiric strength...

...the means to defeat Dracula himself.

But while the power of her first gift increases with each passing night...

...the second gift has begun losing its potency.

TLAK

The serum is weaker and less satisfying each time I take it...while the other hunger, the true thirst, threatens to--

SIR--?

SORRY, ALFRED ...I WAS JUST... THINKING.

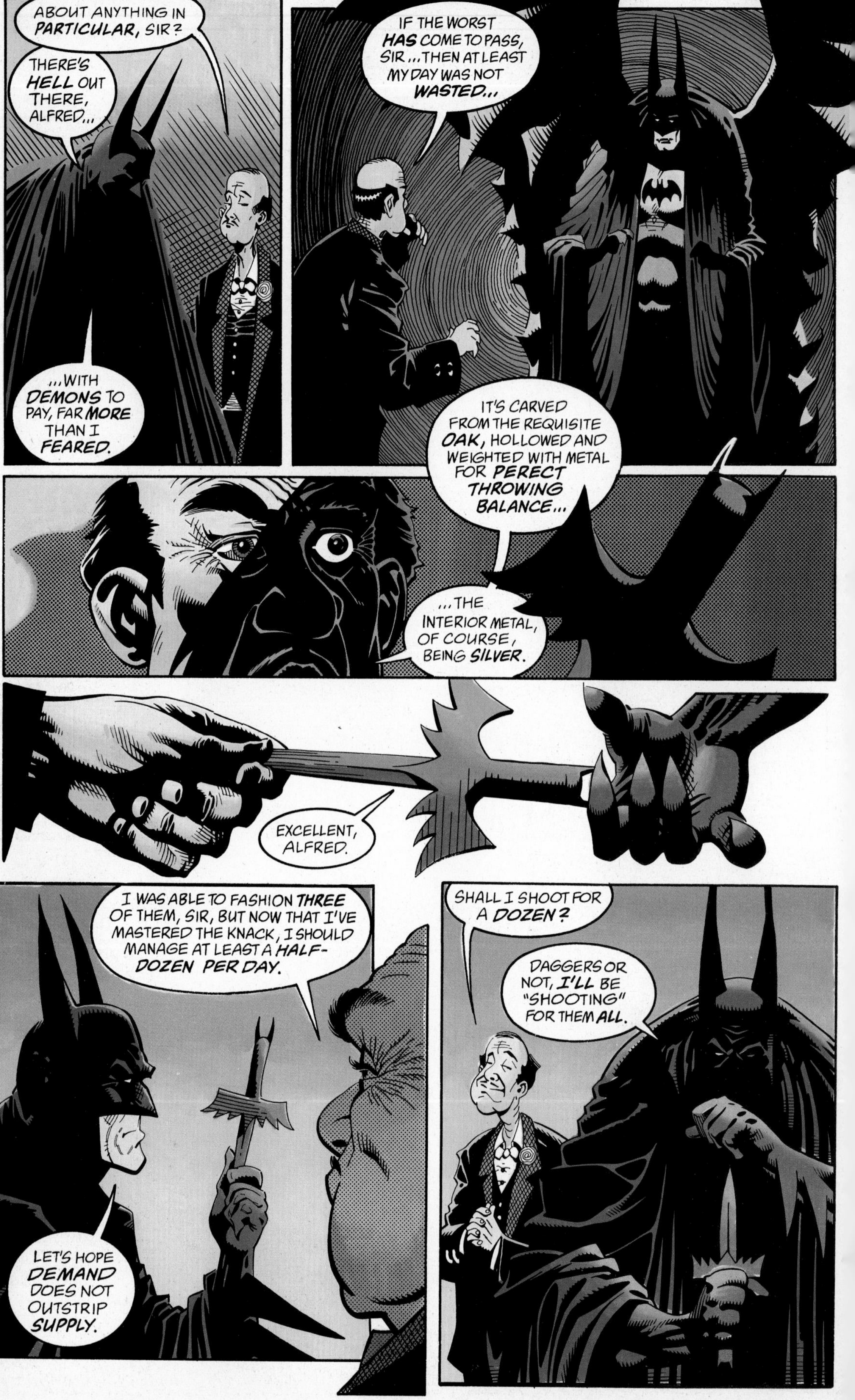
ABOUT ANYTHING IN PARTICULAR, SIR?
THERE'S HELL OUT THERE, ALFRED...
...WITH DEMONS TO PAY, FAR MORE THAN I FEARED.
IF THE WORST HAS COME TO PASS, SIR... THEN AT LEAST MY DAY WAS NOT WASTED...
IT'S CARVED FROM THE REQUISITE OAK, HOLLOWED AND WEIGHTED WITH METAL FOR PERECT THROWING BALANCE...
...THE INTERIOR METAL, OF COURSE, BEING SILVER.
EXCELLENT, ALFRED.
I WAS ABLE TO FASHION THREE OF THEM, SIR, BUT NOW THAT I'VE MASTERED THE KNACK, I SHOULD MANAGE AT LEAST A HALF-DOZEN PER DAY.
LET'S HOPE DEMAND DOES NOT OUTSTRIP SUPPLY.
SHALL I SHOOT FOR A DOZEN?
DAGGERS OR NOT, I'LL BE "SHOOTING" FOR THEM ALL.

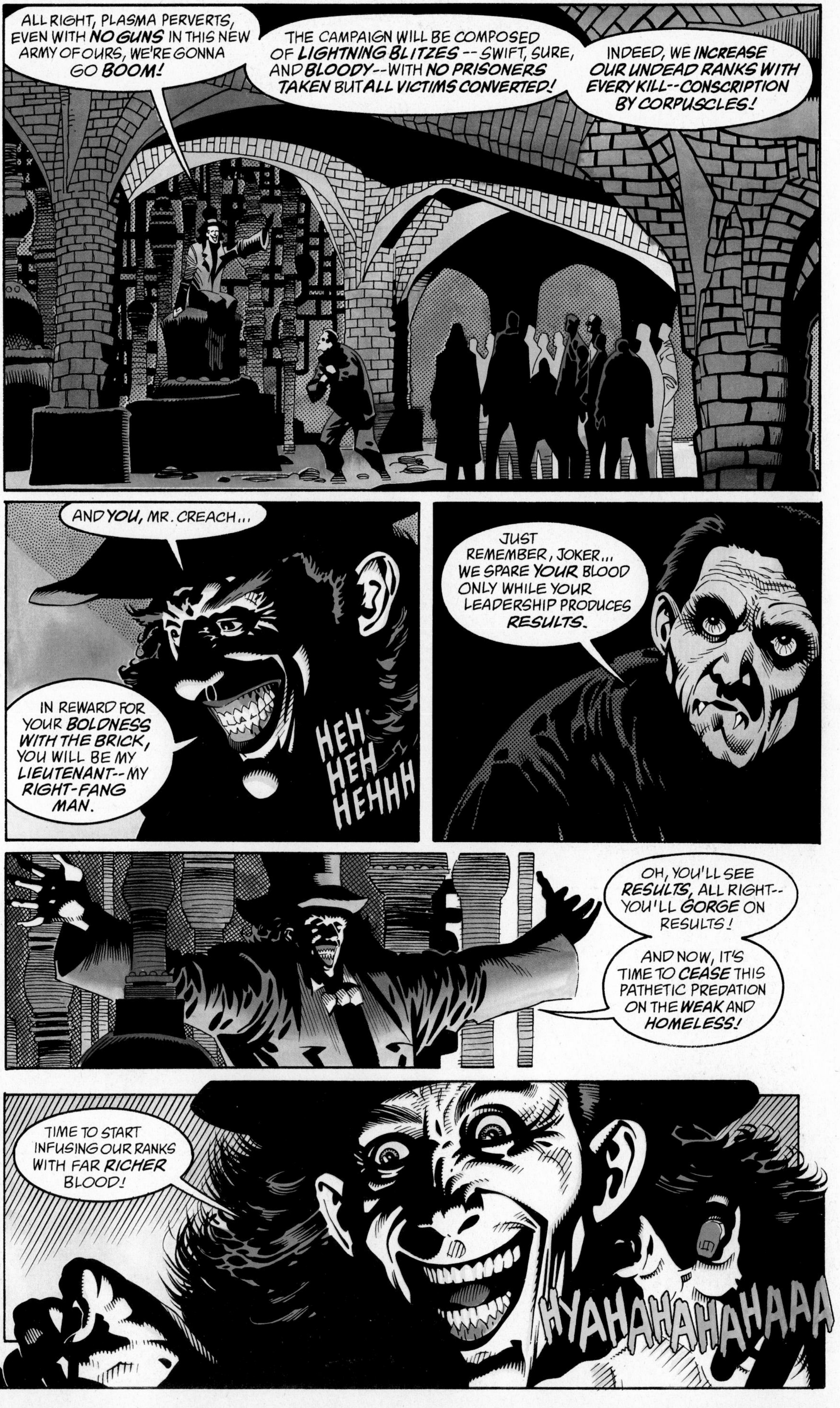
ALL RIGHT, PLASMA PERVERTS, EVEN WITH NO GUNS IN THIS NEW ARMY OF OURS, WE'RE GONNA GO BOOM!
THE CAMPAIGN WILL BE COMPOSED OF LIGHTNING BLITZES -- SWIFT, SURE, AND BLOODY--WITH NO PRISONERS TAKEN BUT ALL VICTIMS CONVERTED!
INDEED, WE INCREASE OUR UNDEAD RANKS WITH EVERY KILL--CONSCRIPTION BY CORPUSCLES!
AND YOU, MR. CREACH...
IN REWARD FOR YOUR BOLDNESS WITH THE BRICK, YOU WILL BE MY LIEUTENANT--MY RIGHT-FANG MAN.
HEH HEH HEHHH
JUST REMEMBER, JOKER... WE SPARE YOUR BLOOD ONLY WHILE YOUR LEADERSHIP PRODUCES RESULTS.
OH, YOU'LL SEE RESULTS, ALL RIGHT-- YOU'LL GORGE ON RESULTS!
AND NOW, IT'S TIME TO CEASE THIS PATHETIC PREDATION ON THE WEAK AND HOMELESS!
TIME TO START INFUSING OUR RANKS WITH FAR RICHER BLOOD!
HYAHAHAHAHAHAAA

MNN...
NHNNN...

WH-WHAT...?

TANYA!
YOU... YOU'RE
BACK?!

YESSS...

BUT... *HOW?*

HUSH...
IT IS
ENOUGH
THAT I AM
HERE.

Y-YES...

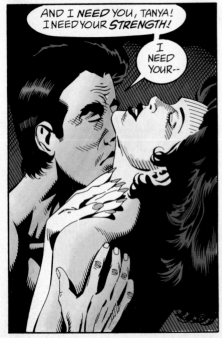

AND I *NEED* YOU, TANYA!
I NEED YOUR *STRENGTH!*

I
NEED
YOUR--

--*BLOOD!*

AUGH-K-K!

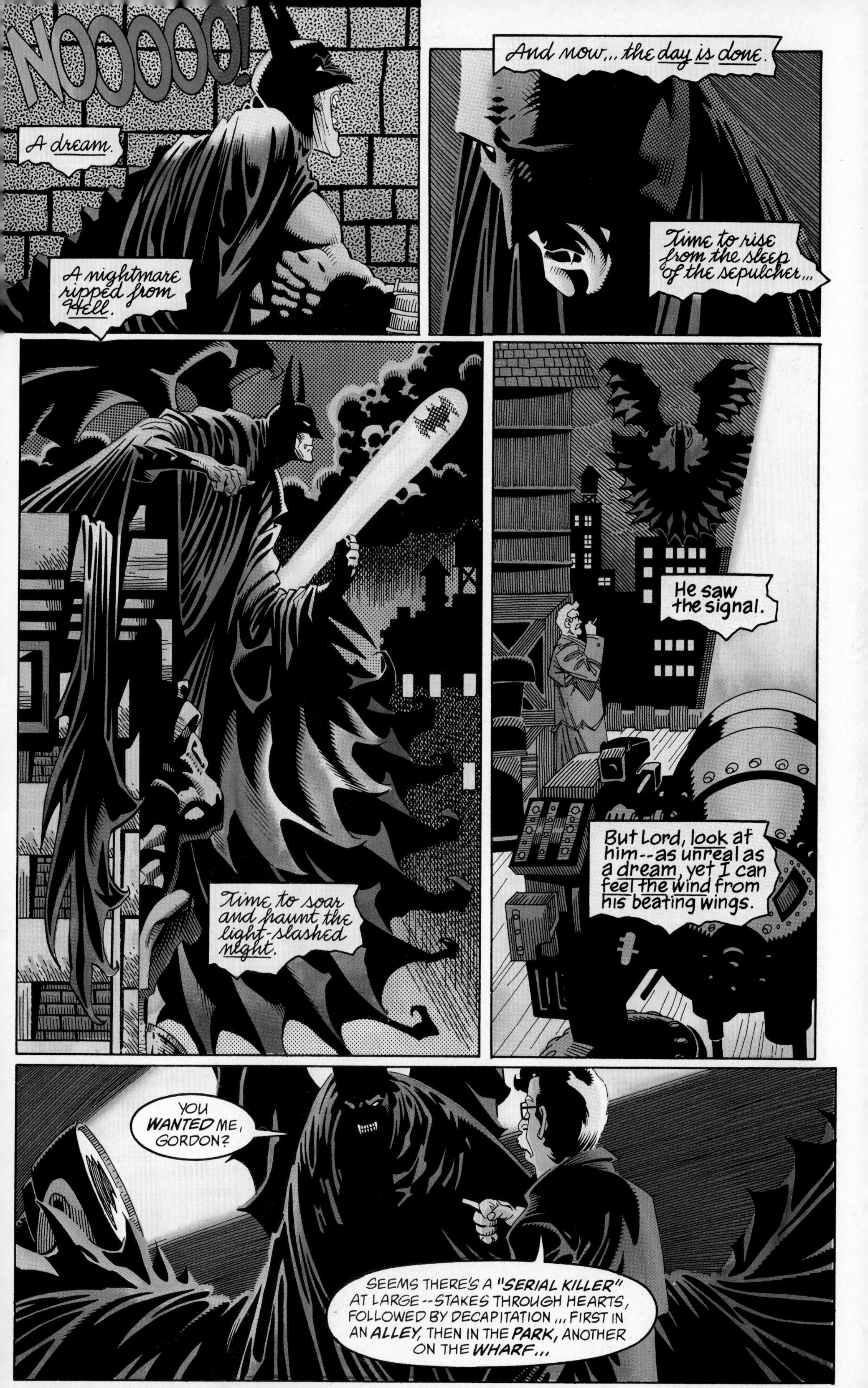
NOOOOO!
A dream.
A nightmare ripped from Hell.
And now... the day is done.
Time to rise from the sleep of the sepulcher...
Time to soar and haunt the light-slashed night.
He saw the signal.
But Lord, look at him--as unreal as a dream, yet I can feel the wind from his beating wings.
YOU WANTED ME, GORDON?
SEEMS THERE'S A "SERIAL KILLER" AT LARGE--STAKES THROUGH HEARTS, FOLLOWED BY DECAPITATION... FIRST IN AN ALLEY, THEN IN THE PARK, ANOTHER ON THE WHARF...

AND IT WON'T STOP *THERE*, GORDON.

TANYA AND *I MISSED* SOME OF THEM.

IF I CAN'T HUNT THE REST BY *NIGHT*, I MAY NEED *DAYLIGHT HELP*.

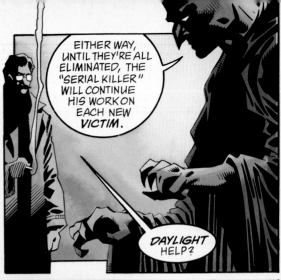

EITHER WAY, UNTIL THEY'RE ALL ELIMINATED, THE "SERIAL KILLER" WILL CONTINUE HIS WORK ON EACH NEW *VICTIM*.

DAYLIGHT HELP?

ENTIRE NESTS OF THE UNDEAD CAN BE TAKEN OUT WHILE THEY *SLEEP*.

I WAS *AFRAID* OF THIS... AFRAID IT WAS... *REAL*.

YOU WERE *THERE*, GORDON-- DRACULA HIMSELF ALMOST *KILLED* YOU.

STILL SEEMS LIKE SOME... BAD DREAM.

A *NIGHTMARE*, BUT *NO DREAM*.

IF I *DO* NEED YOU, CAN YOU *HANDLE* IT?

I'LL PUT TOGETHER A SMALL TEAM... PEOPLE I CAN *TRUST*...

GOOD.

LET'S HOPE IT DOESN'T *COME* TO THAT.

Amen...

...because it'll take more than trust to smash wood through pale things sleeping in coffins and sewers.

KLATCH

More than trust and more than terror... maybe even more than love.

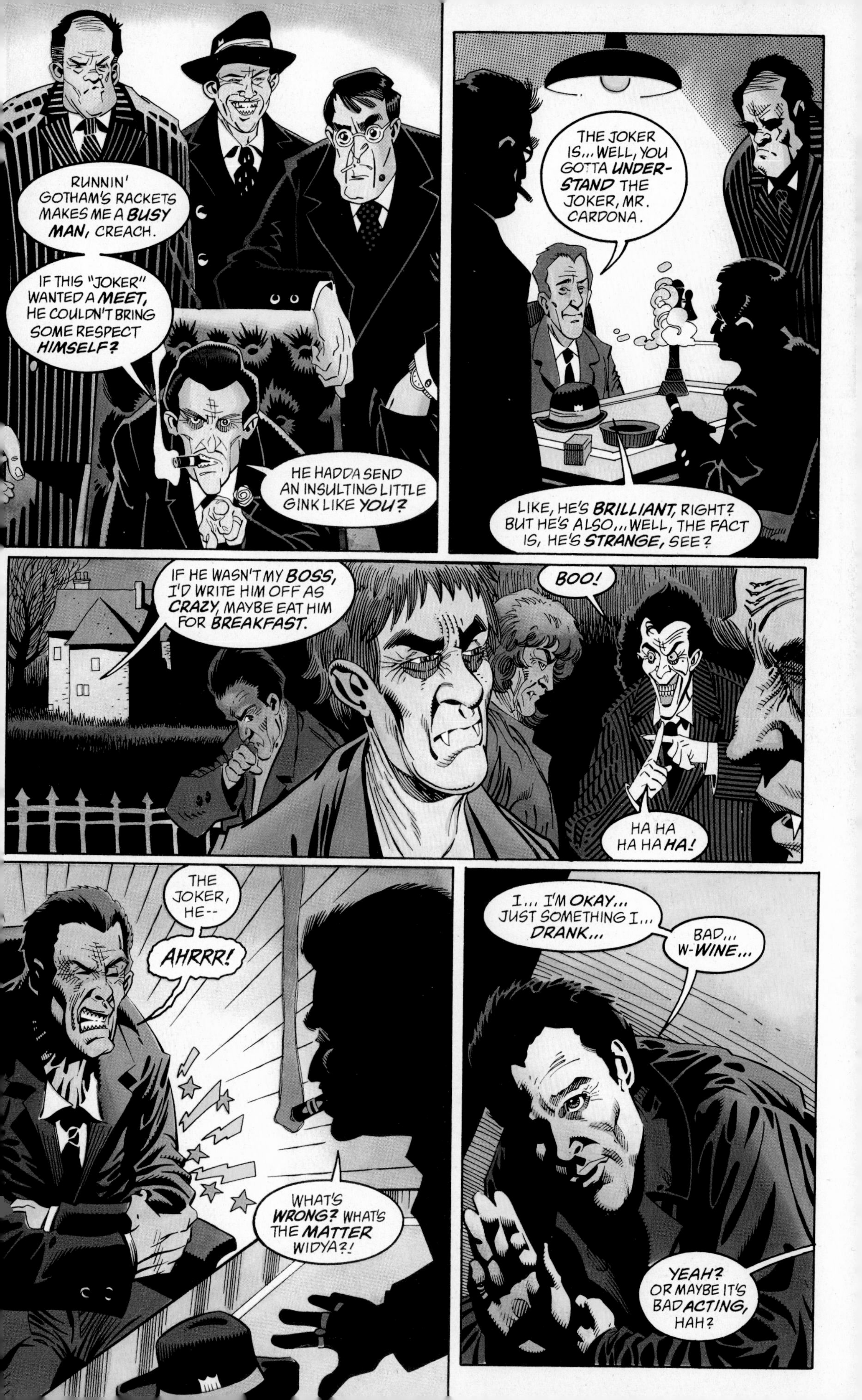
RUNNIN' GOTHAM'S RACKETS MAKES ME A BUSY MAN, CREACH.
IF THIS "JOKER" WANTED A MEET, HE COULDN'T BRING SOME RESPECT HIMSELF?
HE HADDA SEND AN INSULTING LITTLE GINK LIKE YOU?
THE JOKER IS... WELL, YOU GOTTA UNDER-STAND THE JOKER, MR. CARDONA.
LIKE, HE'S BRILLIANT, RIGHT? BUT HE'S ALSO... WELL, THE FACT IS, HE'S STRANGE, SEE?
IF HE WASN'T MY BOSS, I'D WRITE HIM OFF AS CRAZY, MAYBE EAT HIM FOR BREAKFAST.
BOO!
HA HA HA HA HA!
THE JOKER, HE--
AHRRR!
WHAT'S WRONG? WHAT'S THE MATTER WIDYA?!
I... I'M OKAY... JUST SOMETHING I... DRANK...
BAD... W-WINE...
YEAH? OR MAYBE IT'S BAD ACTING, HAH?

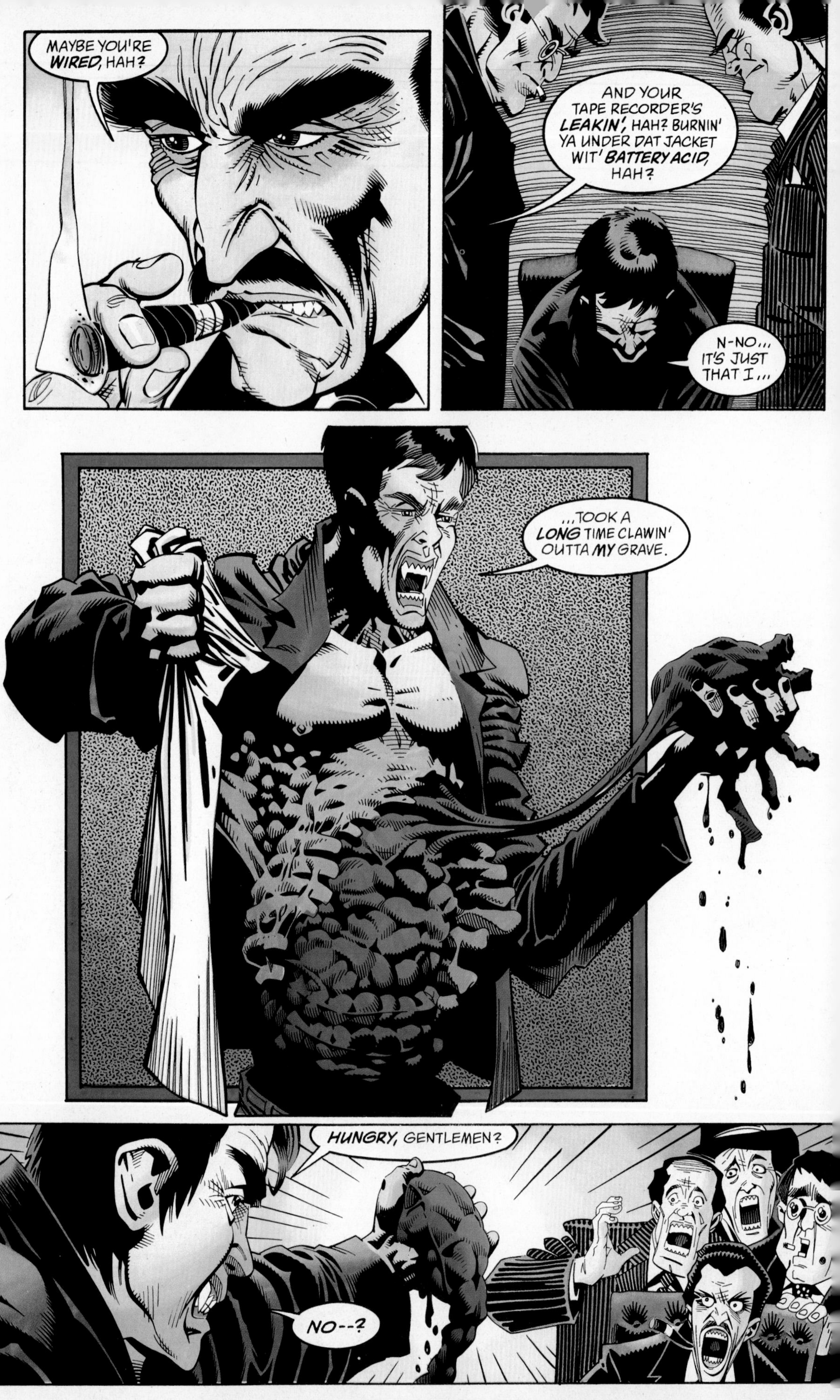
MAYBE YOU'RE WIRED, HAH?
AND YOUR TAPE RECORDER'S LEAKIN', HAH? BURNIN' YA UNDER DAT JACKET WIT' BATTERY ACID, HAH?
N-NO... IT'S JUST THAT I...
...TOOK A LONG TIME CLAWIN' OUTTA MY GRAVE.
HUNGRY, GENTLEMEN?
NO--?

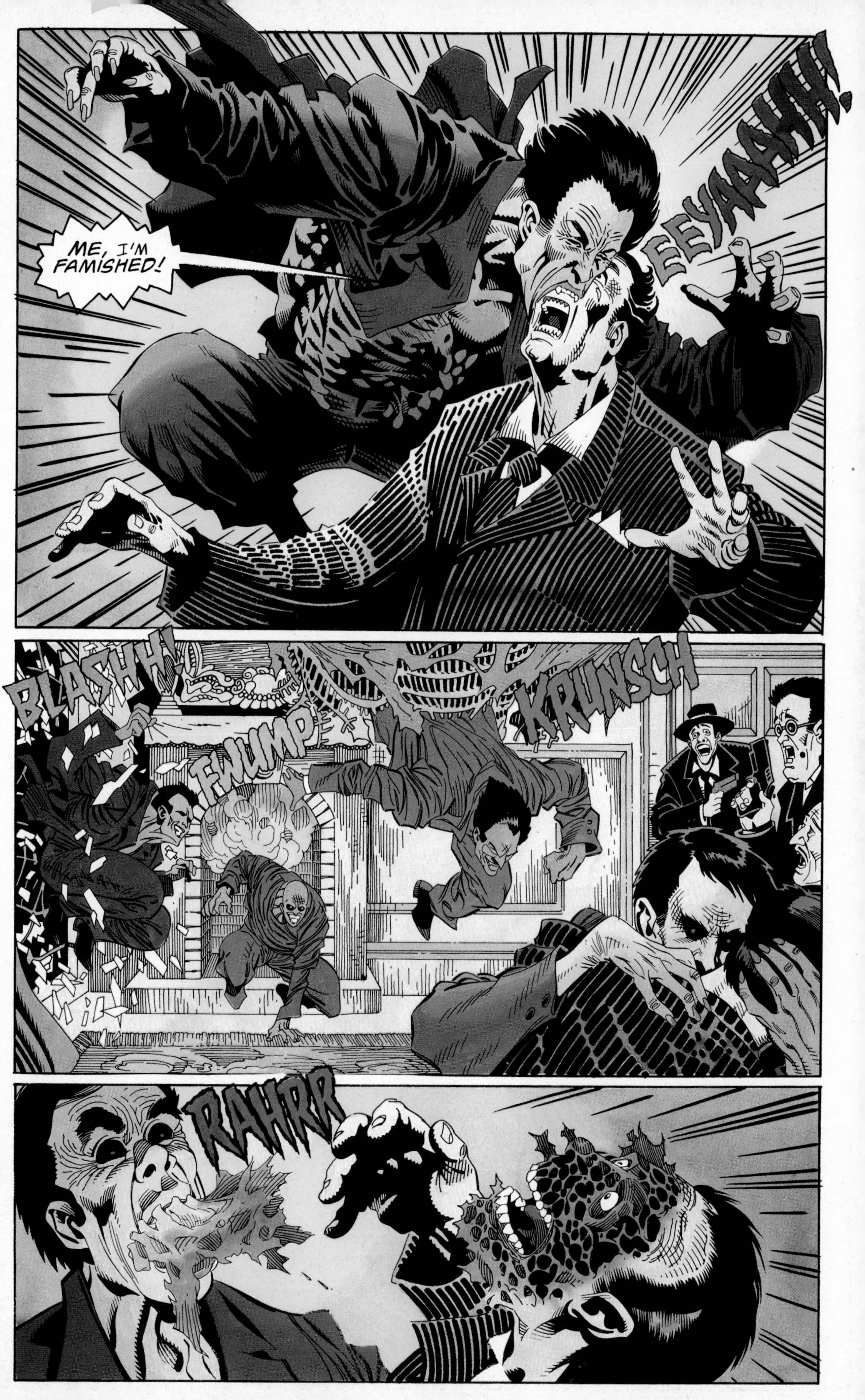
ME, I'M FAMISHED!
EEYAAAHH!!
BLASHH!
FWUMP
KRUNSCH
RAHRR

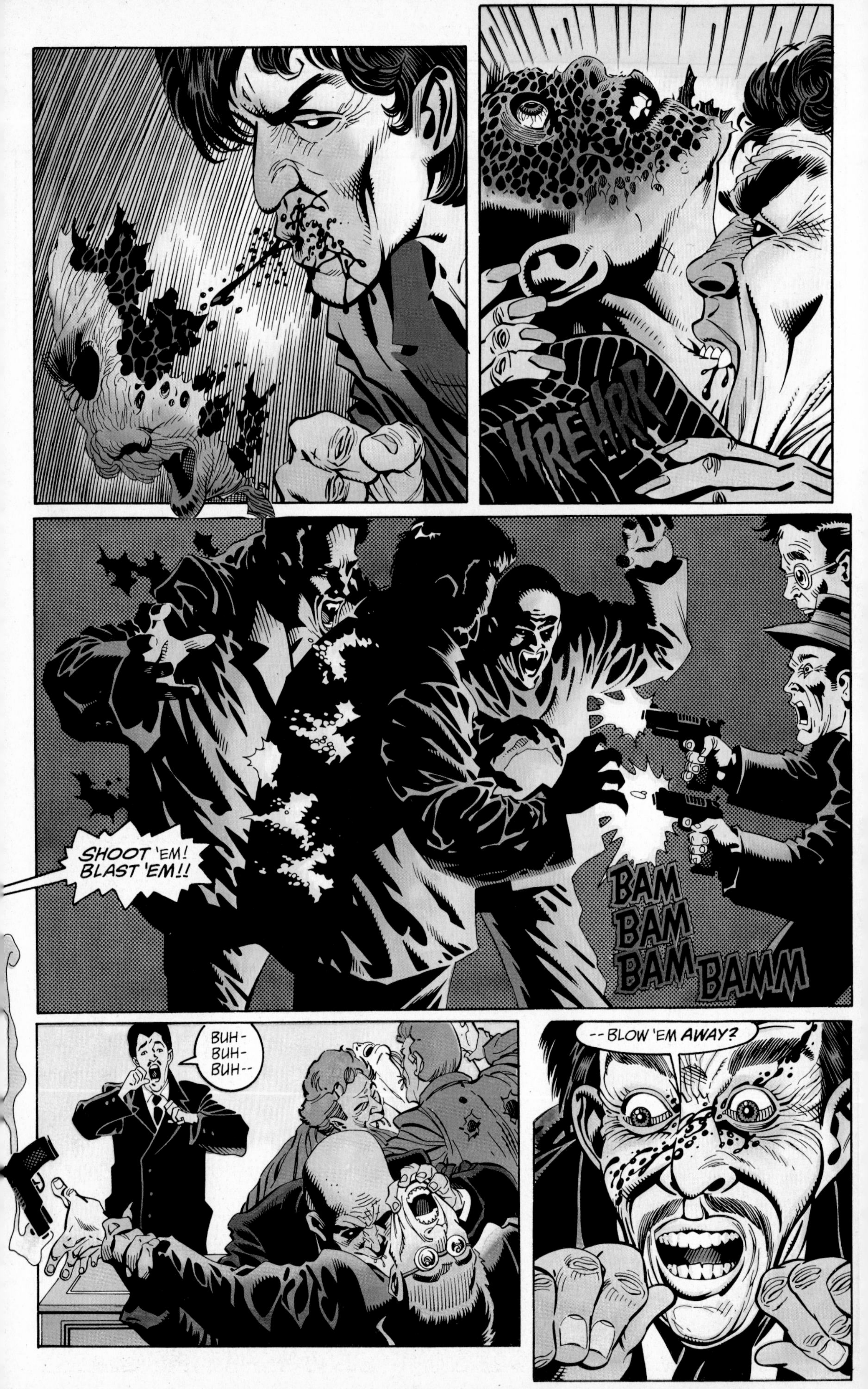
HREHRR
SHOOT 'EM! BLAST 'EM!!
BAM BAM BAM BAMM
BUH- BUH- BUH--
--BLOW 'EM AWAY?

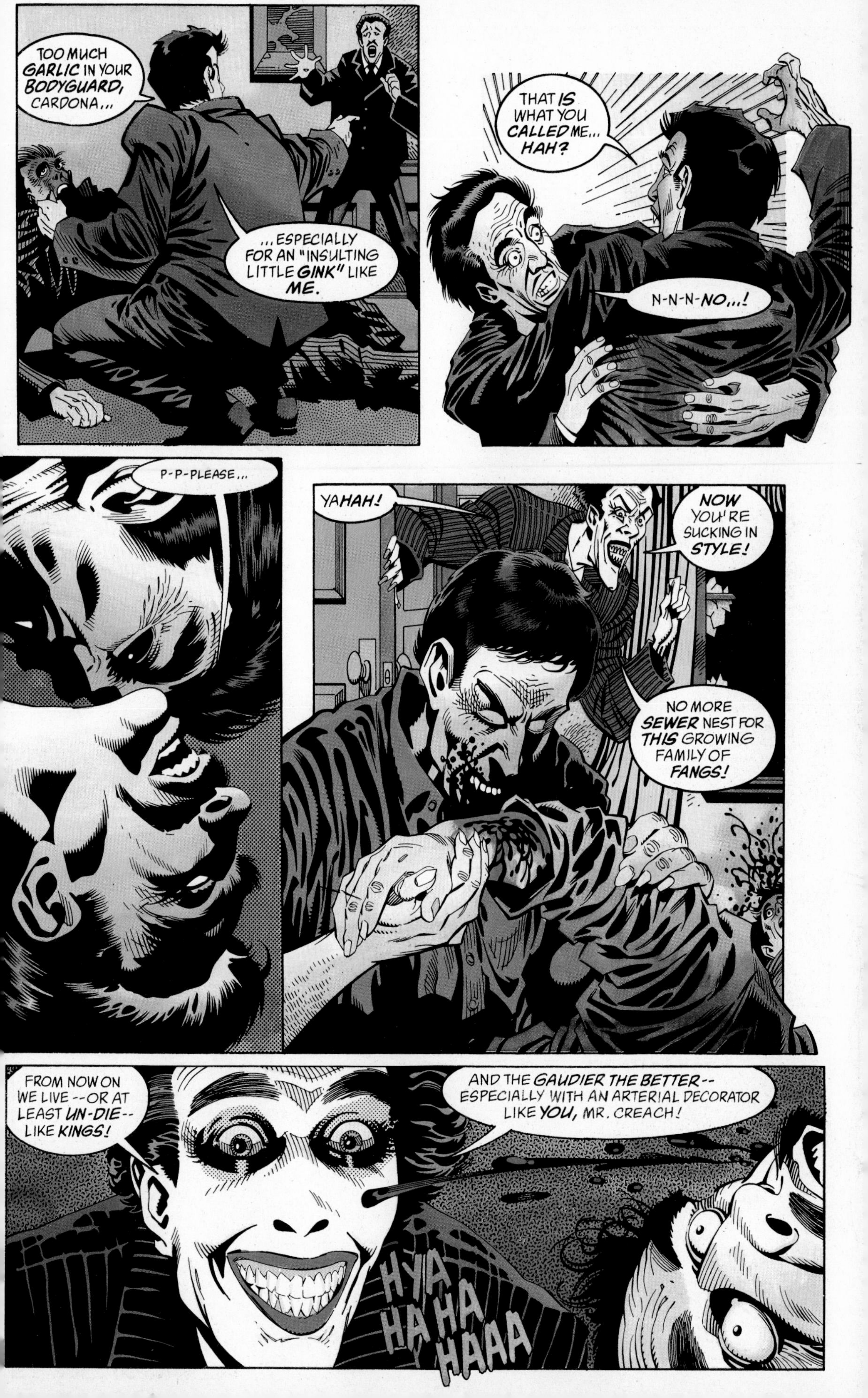
TOO MUCH GARLIC IN YOUR BODYGUARD, CARDONA...
...ESPECIALLY FOR AN "INSULTING LITTLE GINK" LIKE ME.
THAT IS WHAT YOU CALLED ME... HAH?
N-N-N-NO...!
P-P-PLEASE...
YAHAH!
NOW YOU'RE SUCKING IN STYLE!
NO MORE SEWER NEST FOR THIS GROWING FAMILY OF FANGS!
FROM NOW ON WE LIVE--OR AT LEAST UN-DIE-- LIKE KINGS!
AND THE GAUDIER THE BETTER-- ESPECIALLY WITH AN ARTERIAL DECORATOR LIKE YOU, MR. CREACH!
HYA HA HA HAAA

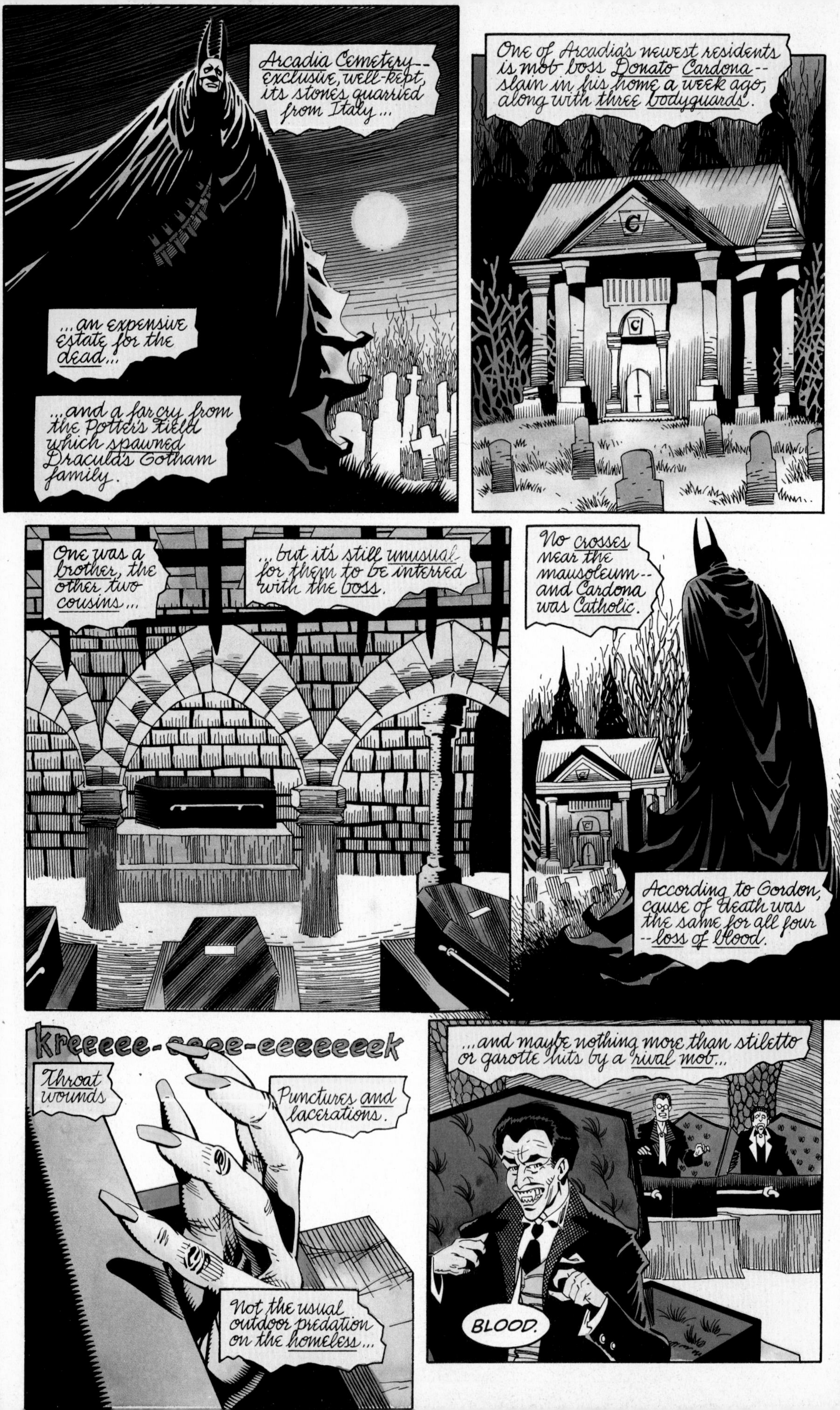
Arcadia Cemetery-- exclusive, well-kept, its stones quarried from Italy...
...an expensive estate for the dead...
...and a far cry from the Potter's Field which spawned Dracula's Gotham family.
One of Arcadia's newest residents is mob boss Donato Cardona-- slain in his home a week ago, along with three bodyguards.
One was a brother, the other two cousins...
...but it's still unusual for them to be interred with the boss.
No crosses near the mausoleum-- and Cardona was Catholic.
According to Gordon, cause of death was the same for all four --loss of blood.
kreeeee-eeee-eeeeeeek
Throat wounds
Punctures and lacerations.
Not the usual outdoor predation on the homeless...
...and maybe nothing more than stiletto or garotte hits by a rival mob...
BLOOD.

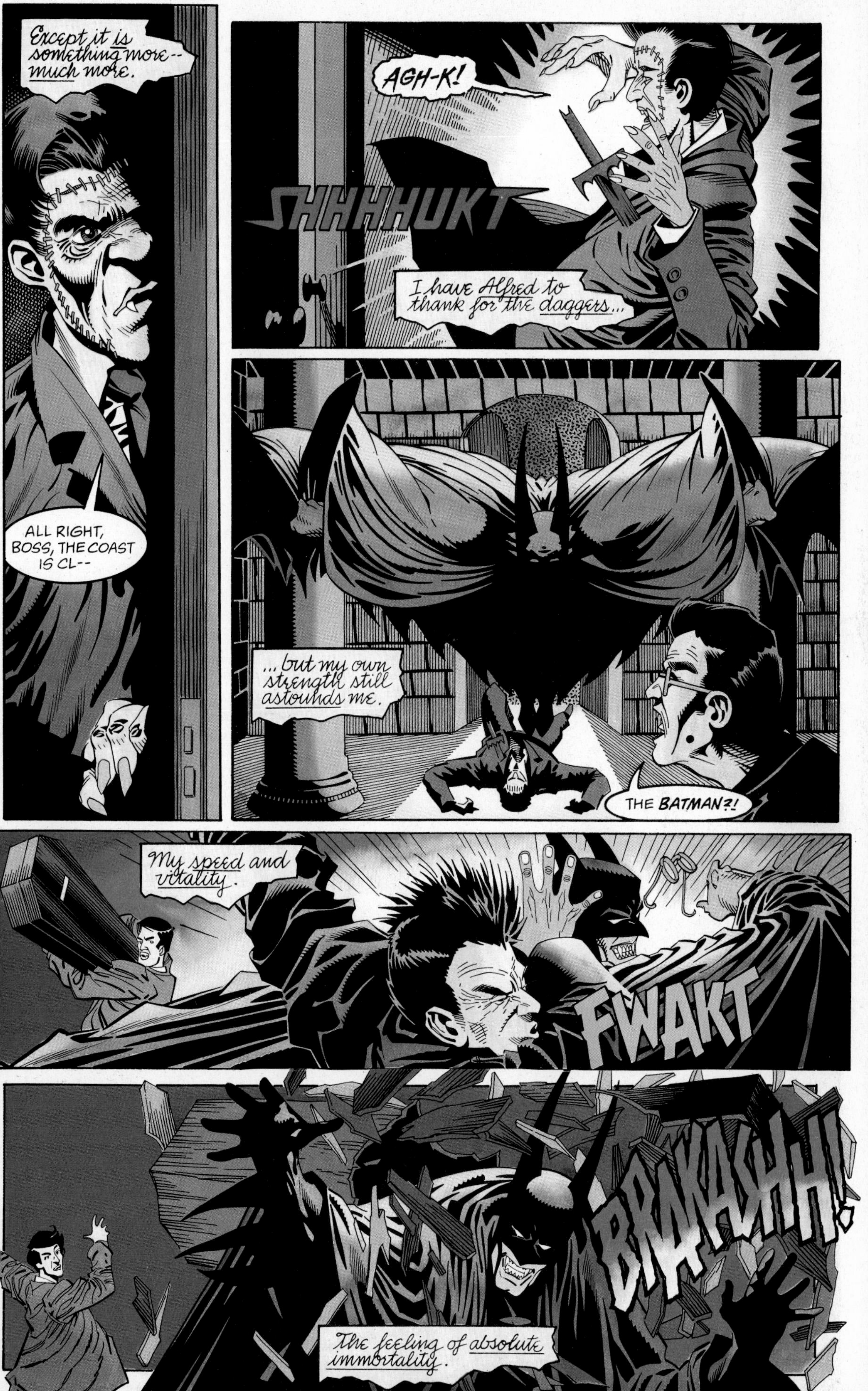
Except it is something more-- much more.
AGH-K!
SHHHHUKT
I have Alfred to thank for the daggers...
ALL RIGHT, BOSS, THE COAST IS CL--
...but my own strength still astounds me.
THE BATMAN?!
My speed and vitality.
FWAKT
BRAKASHH!
The feeling of absolute immortality.

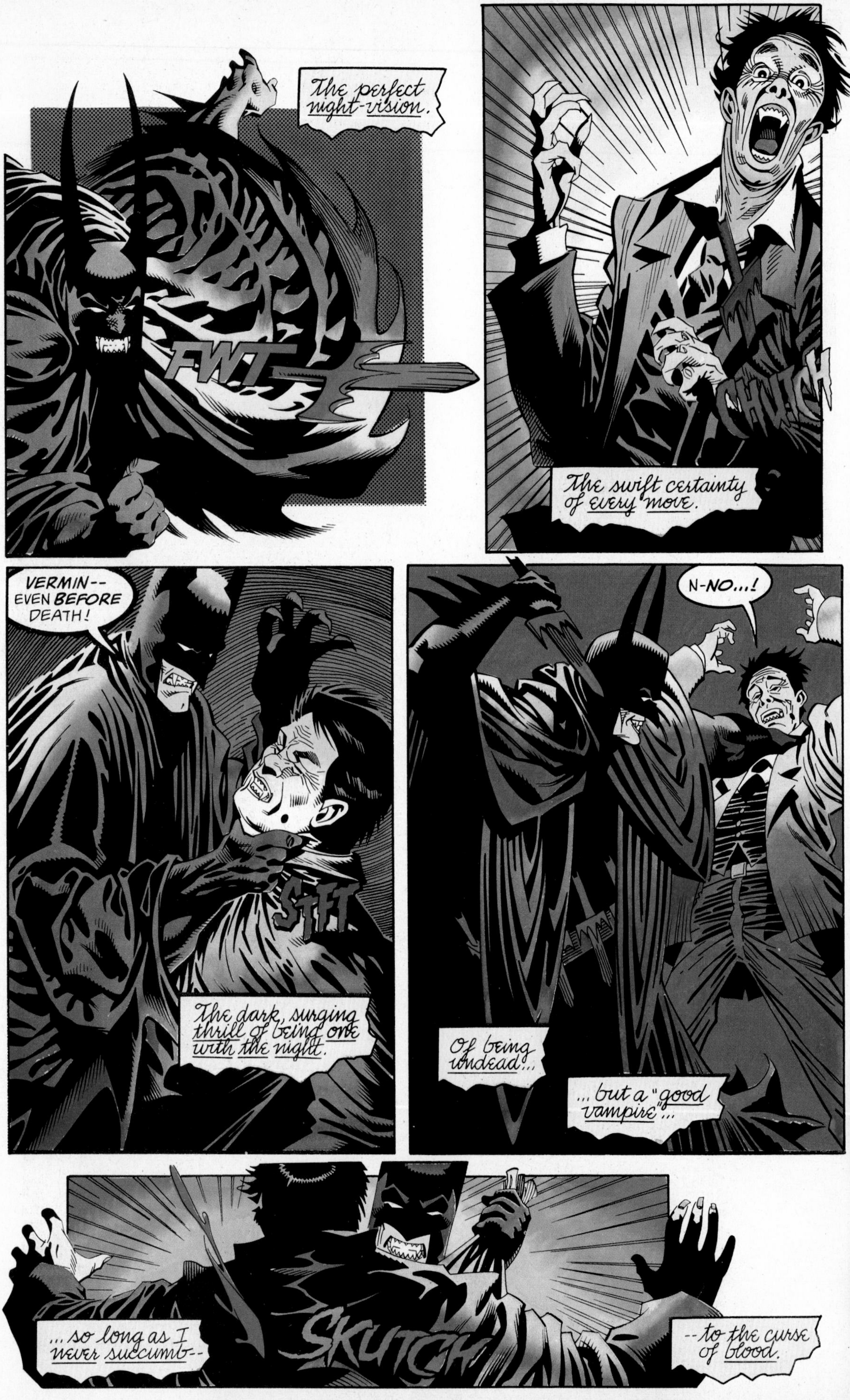
The perfect night-vision.
FWT
CHUTCH
The swift certainty of every move.
VERMIN-- EVEN BEFORE DEATH!
STFT
The dark, surging thrill of being one with the night.
N-NO...!
Of being undead...
...but a "good vampire"...
...so long as I never succumb--
SKUTCH
--to the curse of blood.

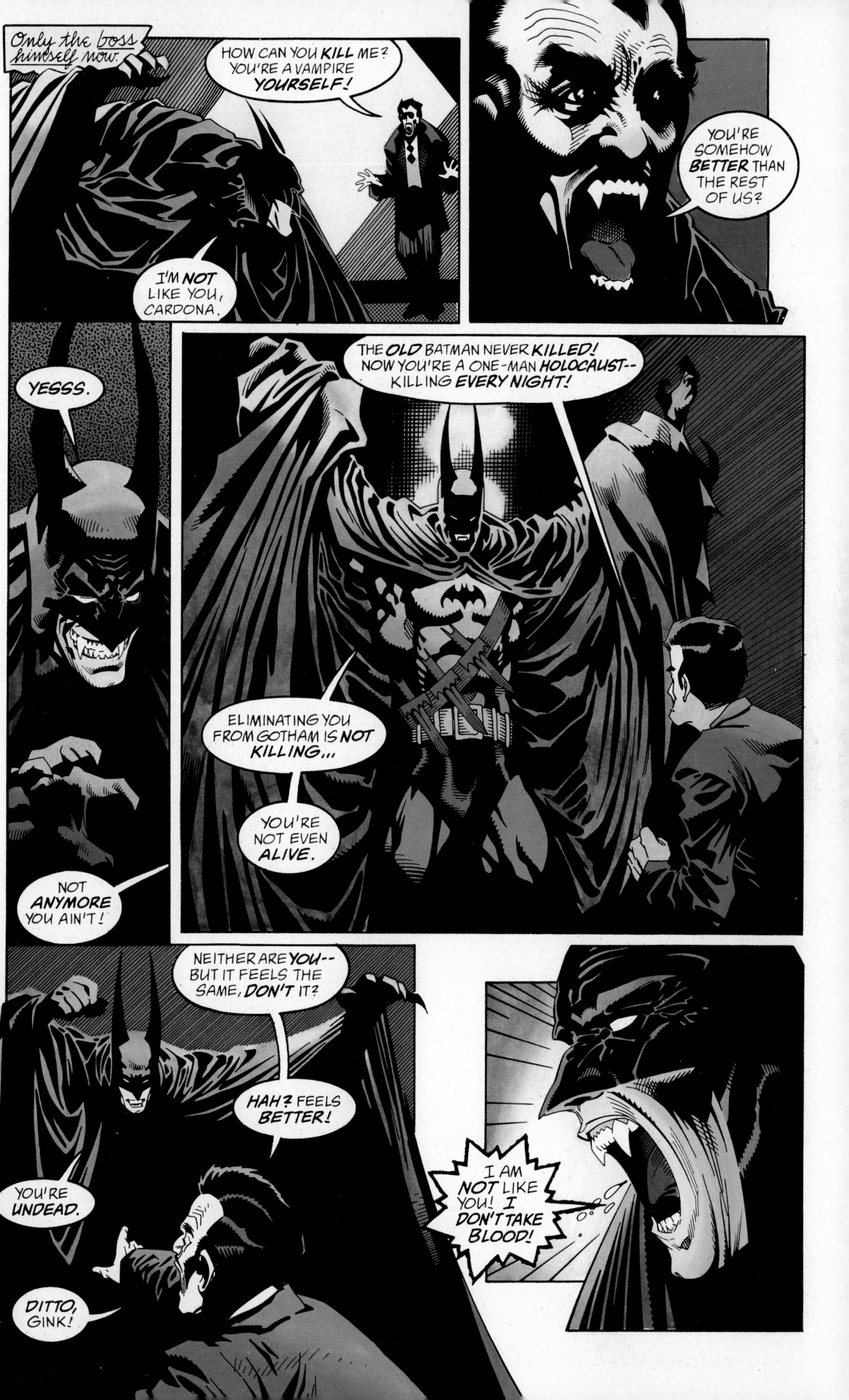

Only the boss himself now.
HOW CAN YOU KILL ME? YOU'RE A VAMPIRE YOURSELF!
I'M NOT LIKE YOU, CARDONA.
YOU'RE SOMEHOW BETTER THAN THE REST OF US?
YESSS.
THE OLD BATMAN NEVER KILLED! NOW YOU'RE A ONE-MAN HOLOCAUST-- KILLING EVERY NIGHT!
ELIMINATING YOU FROM GOTHAM IS NOT KILLING...
YOU'RE NOT EVEN ALIVE.
NOT ANYMORE YOU AIN'T!
NEITHER ARE YOU-- BUT IT FEELS THE SAME, DON'T IT?
HAH? FEELS BETTER!
YOU'RE UNDEAD.
DITTO, GINK!
I AM NOT LIKE YOU! I DON'T TAKE BLOOD!

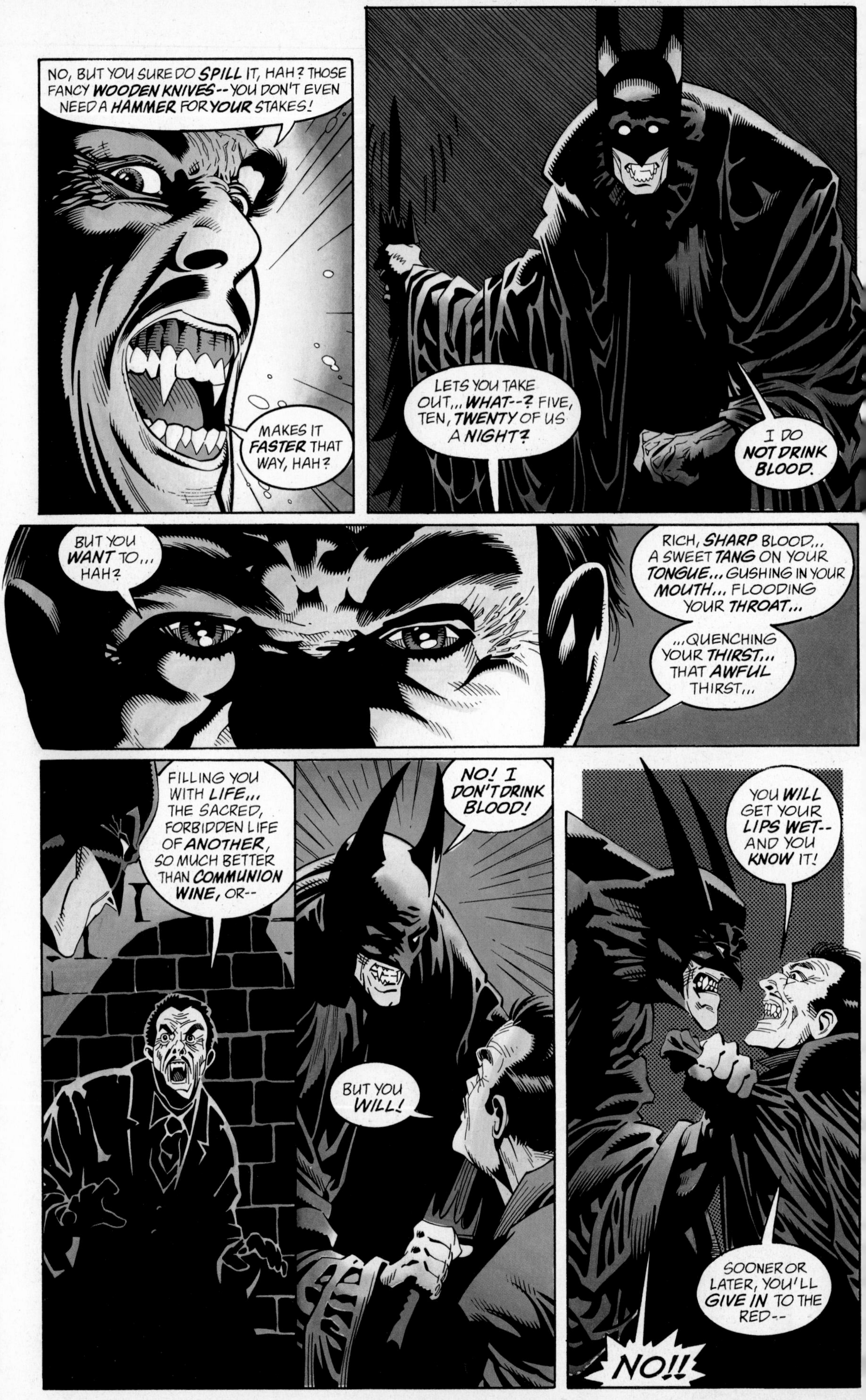

NO, BUT YOU SURE DO SPILL IT, HAH? THOSE FANCY WOODEN KNIVES--YOU DON'T EVEN NEED A HAMMER FOR YOUR STAKES!
MAKES IT FASTER THAT WAY, HAH?
LETS YOU TAKE OUT... WHAT--? FIVE, TEN, TWENTY OF US A NIGHT?
I DO NOT DRINK BLOOD.
BUT YOU WANT TO... HAH?
RICH, SHARP BLOOD... A SWEET TANG ON YOUR TONGUE... GUSHING IN YOUR MOUTH... FLOODING YOUR THROAT...
...QUENCHING YOUR THIRST... THAT AWFUL THIRST...
FILLING YOU WITH LIFE... THE SACRED, FORBIDDEN LIFE OF ANOTHER, SO MUCH BETTER THAN COMMUNION WINE, OR--
NO! I DON'T DRINK BLOOD!
BUT YOU WILL!
YOU WILL GET YOUR LIPS WET-- AND YOU KNOW IT!
SOONER OR LATER, YOU'LL GIVE IN TO THE RED--
NO!!

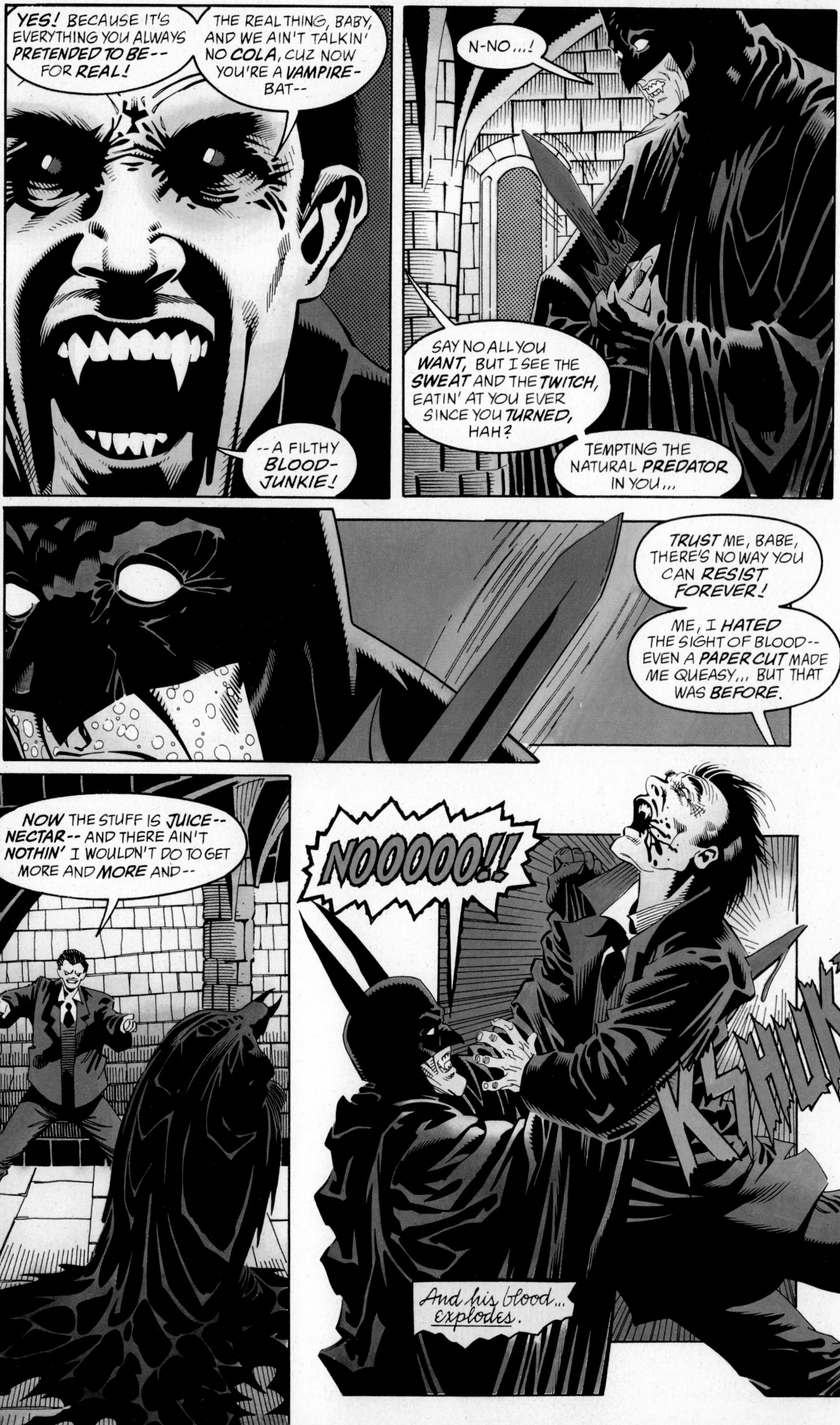
YES! BECAUSE IT'S EVERYTHING YOU ALWAYS PRETENDED TO BE-- FOR REAL!
THE REAL THING, BABY, AND WE AIN'T TALKIN' NO COLA, CUZ NOW YOU'RE A VAMPIRE-BAT--
--A FILTHY BLOOD-JUNKIE!
N-NO...!
SAY NO ALL YOU WANT, BUT I SEE THE SWEAT AND THE TWITCH, EATIN' AT YOU EVER SINCE YOU TURNED, HAH?
TEMPTING THE NATURAL PREDATOR IN YOU...
TRUST ME, BABE, THERE'S NO WAY YOU CAN RESIST FOREVER!
ME, I HATED THE SIGHT OF BLOOD-- EVEN A PAPER CUT MADE ME QUEASY... BUT THAT WAS BEFORE.
NOW THE STUFF IS JUICE-- NECTAR-- AND THERE AIN'T NOTHIN' I WOULDN'T DO TO GET MORE AND MORE AND--
NOOOOO!!
KSHUKT
And his blood... explodes.

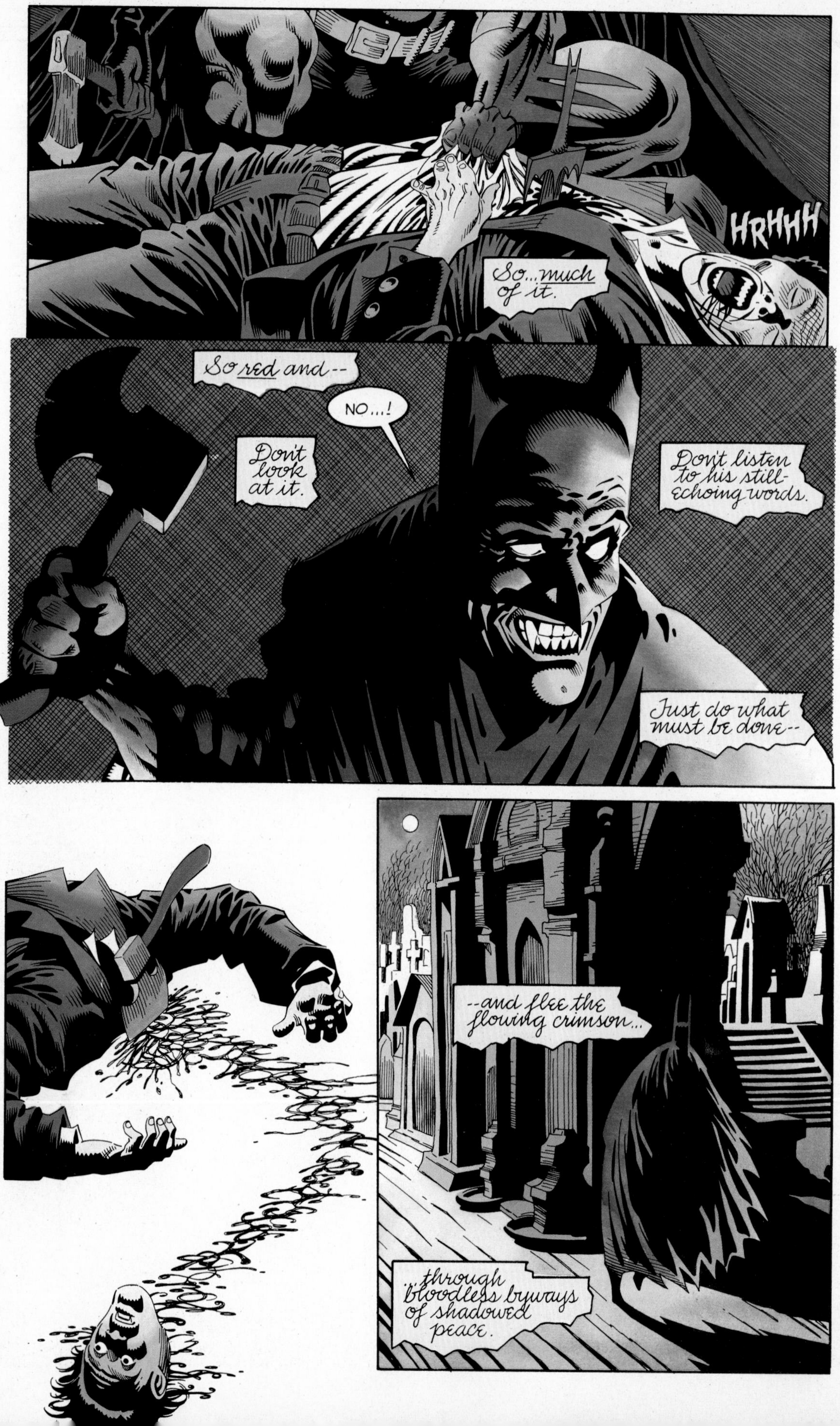

HRHHH
So... much of it.
So red and--
NO...!
Don't look at it.
Don't listen to his still-echoing words.
Just do what must be done--
--and flee the flowing crimson...
...through bloodless byways of shadowed peace.

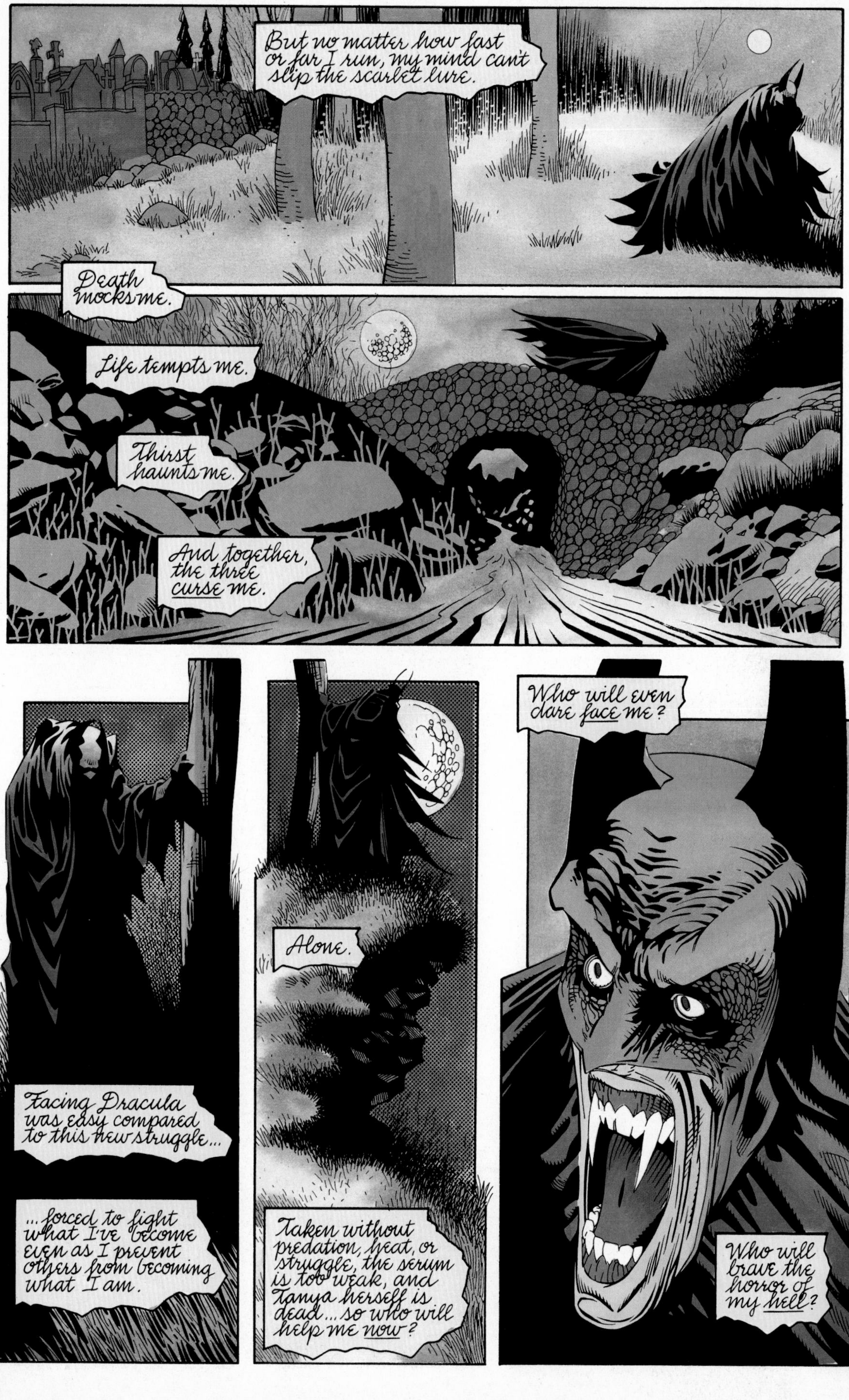
But no matter how fast or far I run, my mind can't slip the scarlet lure.
Death mocks me.
Life tempts me.
Thirst haunts me.
And together, the three curse me.
Facing Dracula was easy compared to this new struggle...
...forced to fight what I've become even as I prevent others from becoming what I am.
Alone.
Taken without predation, heat, or struggle, the serum is too weak, and Tanya herself is dead... so who will help me now?
Who will even dare face me?
Who will brave the horror of my hell?

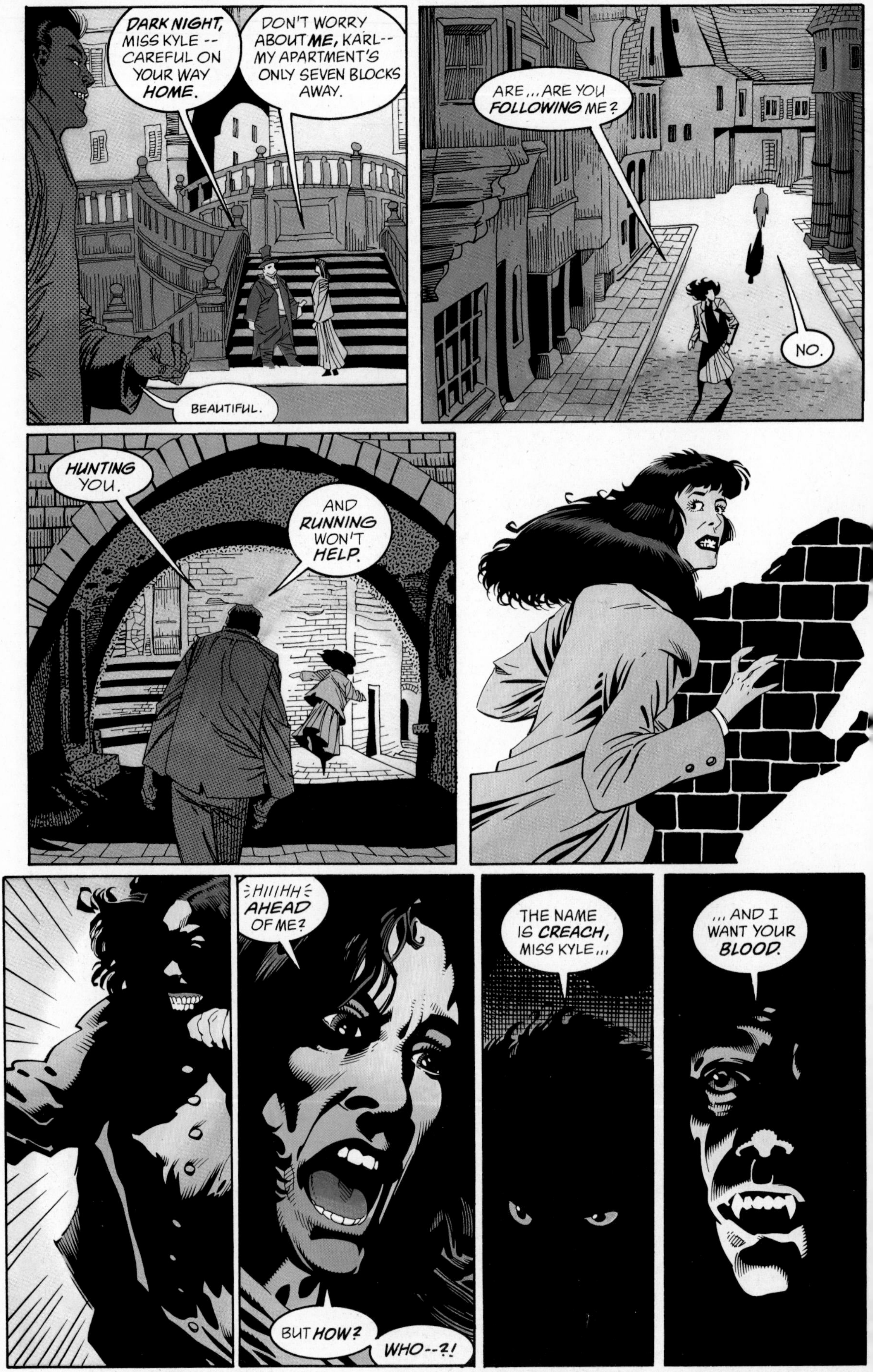
DARK NIGHT, MISS KYLE -- CAREFUL ON YOUR WAY HOME.
DON'T WORRY ABOUT ME, KARL-- MY APARTMENT'S ONLY SEVEN BLOCKS AWAY.
BEAUTIFUL.
ARE... ARE YOU FOLLOWING ME?
NO.
HUNTING YOU.
AND RUNNING WON'T HELP.
HIIIHH
AHEAD OF ME?
BUT HOW?
WHO--?!
THE NAME IS CREACH, MISS KYLE...
...AND I WANT YOUR BLOOD.

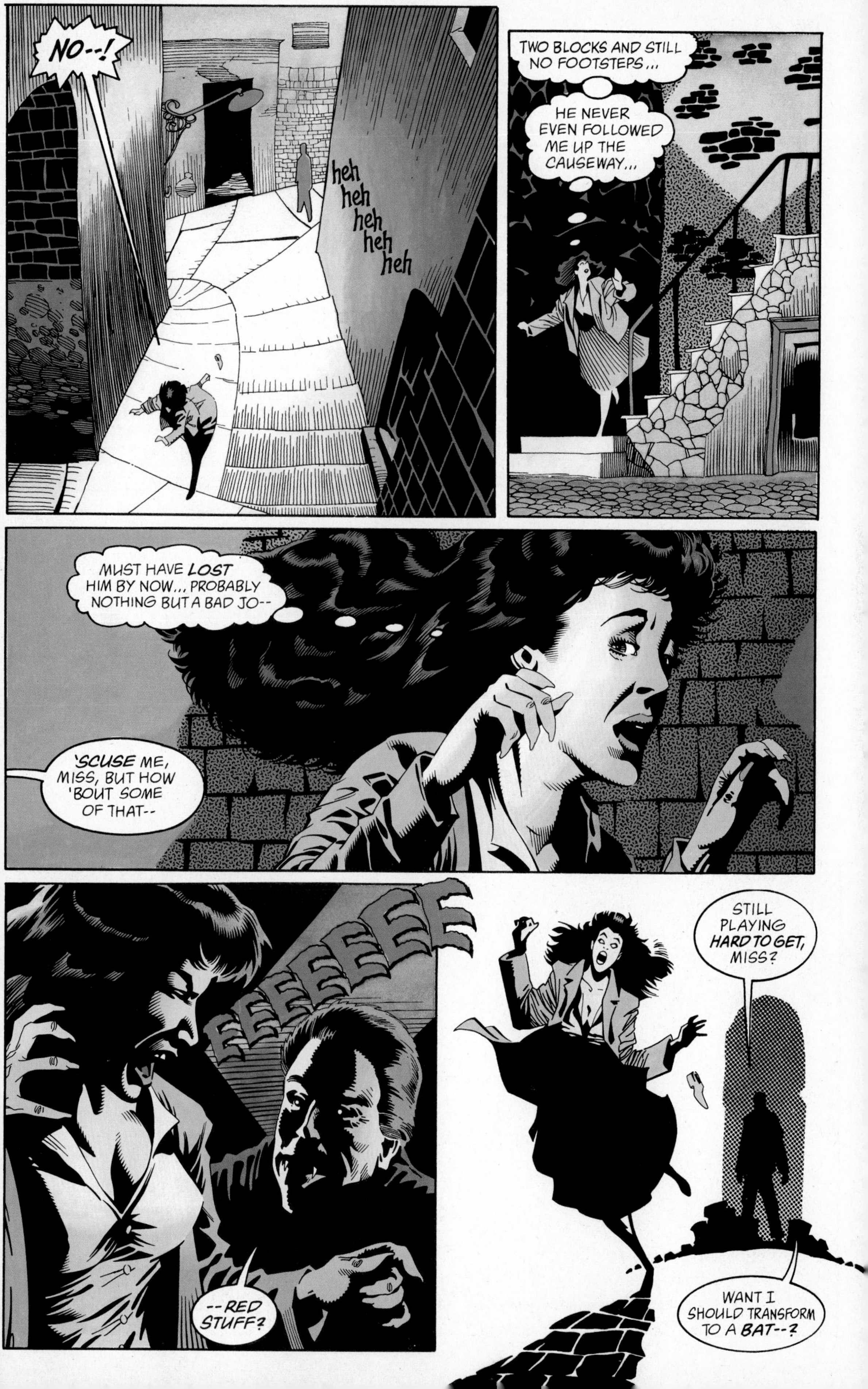
NO--!
heh heh heh heh heh
TWO BLOCKS AND STILL NO FOOTSTEPS...
HE NEVER EVEN FOLLOWED ME UP THE CAUSEWAY...
MUST HAVE LOST HIM BY NOW... PROBABLY NOTHING BUT A BAD JO--
'SCUSE ME, MISS, BUT HOW 'BOUT SOME OF THAT--
EEEEEEE
--RED STUFF?
STILL PLAYING HARD TO GET, MISS?
WANT I SHOULD TRANSFORM TO A BAT--?

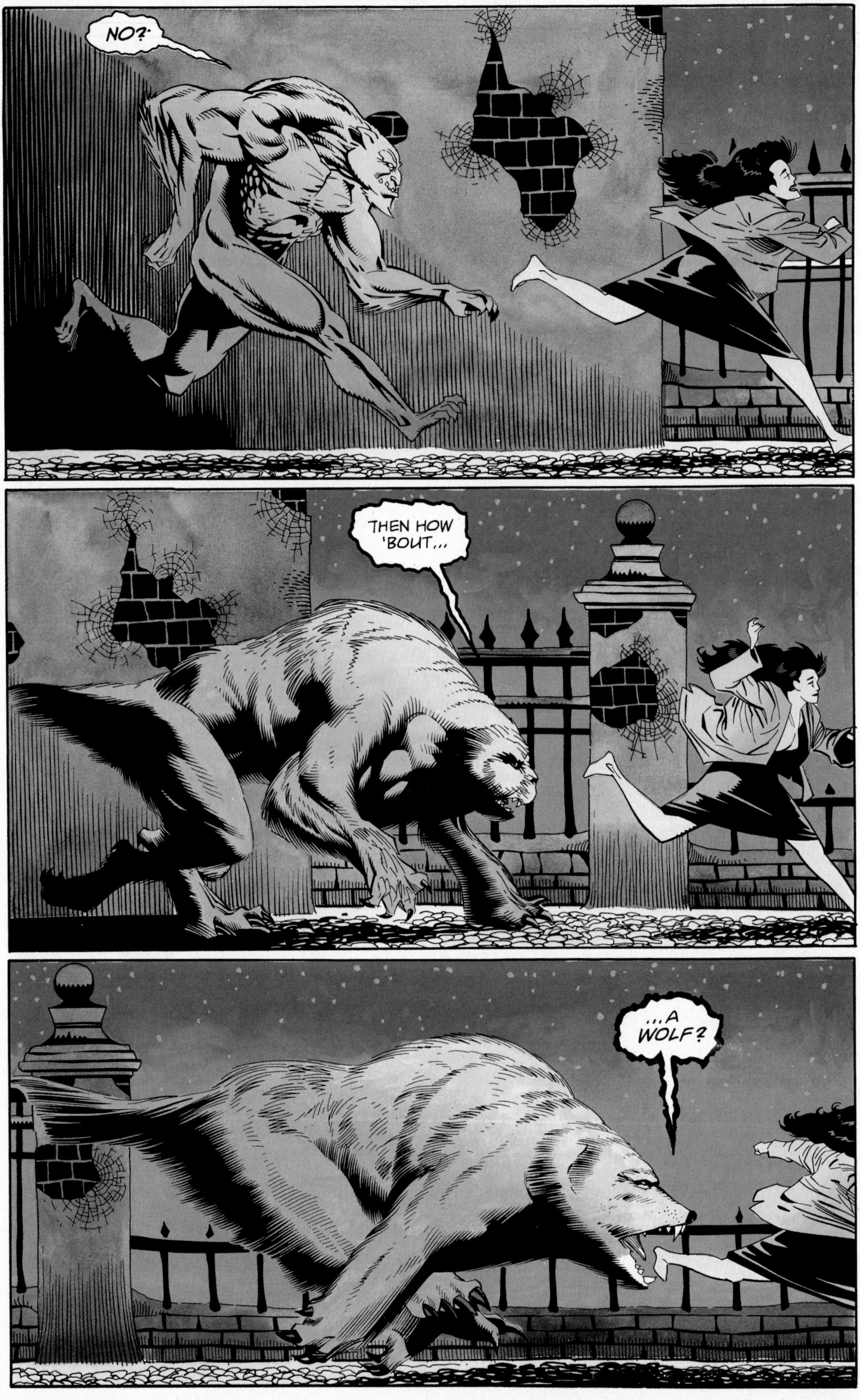
NO?
THEN HOW 'BOUT...
...A WOLF?

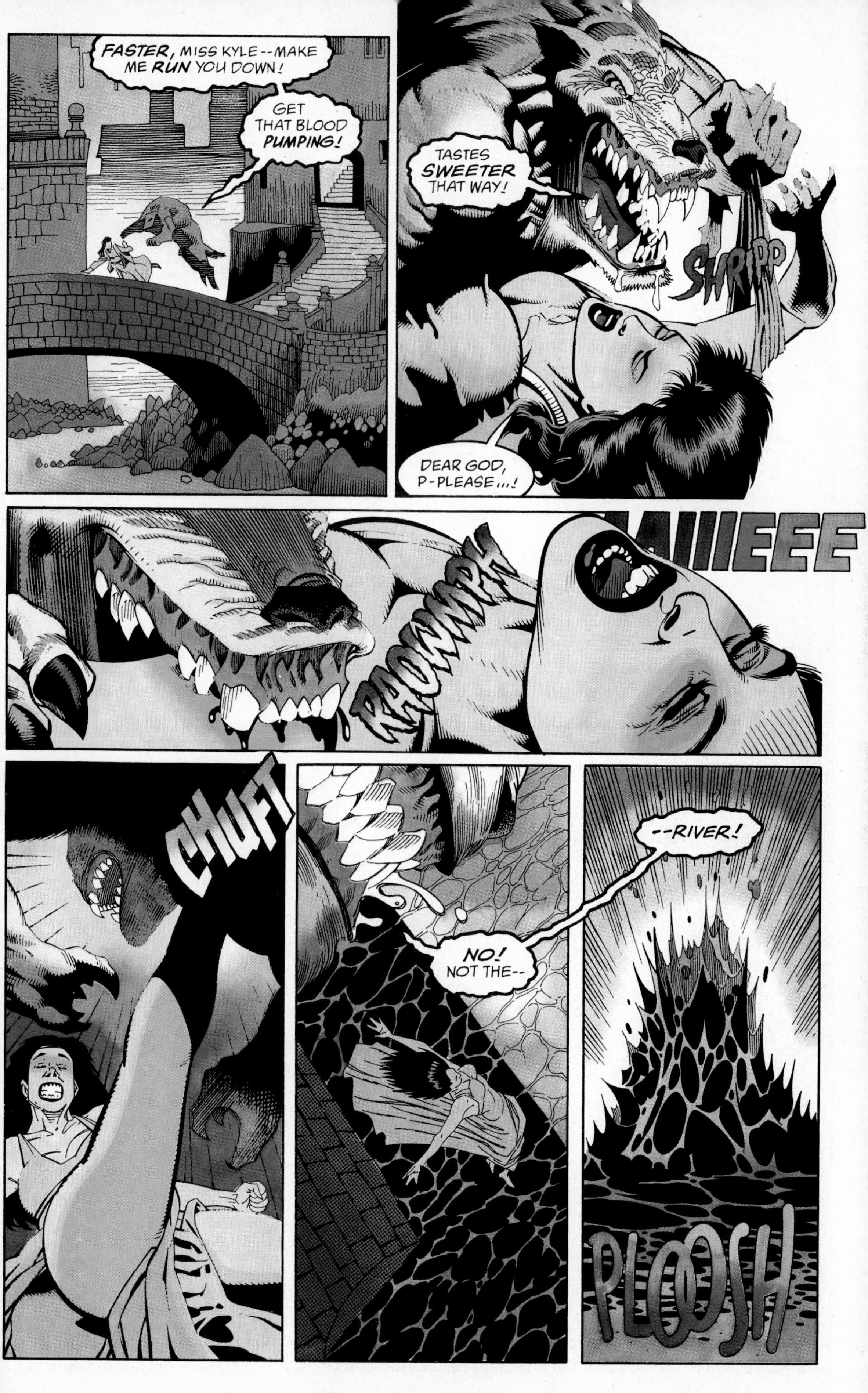
FASTER, MISS KYLE--MAKE ME RUN YOU DOWN!
GET THAT BLOOD PUMPING!
TASTES SWEETER THAT WAY!
SHRIPP
DEAR GOD, P-PLEASE...!
AAIIIEEE
CHUFT
NO! NOT THE--
--RIVER!
PLOOSH

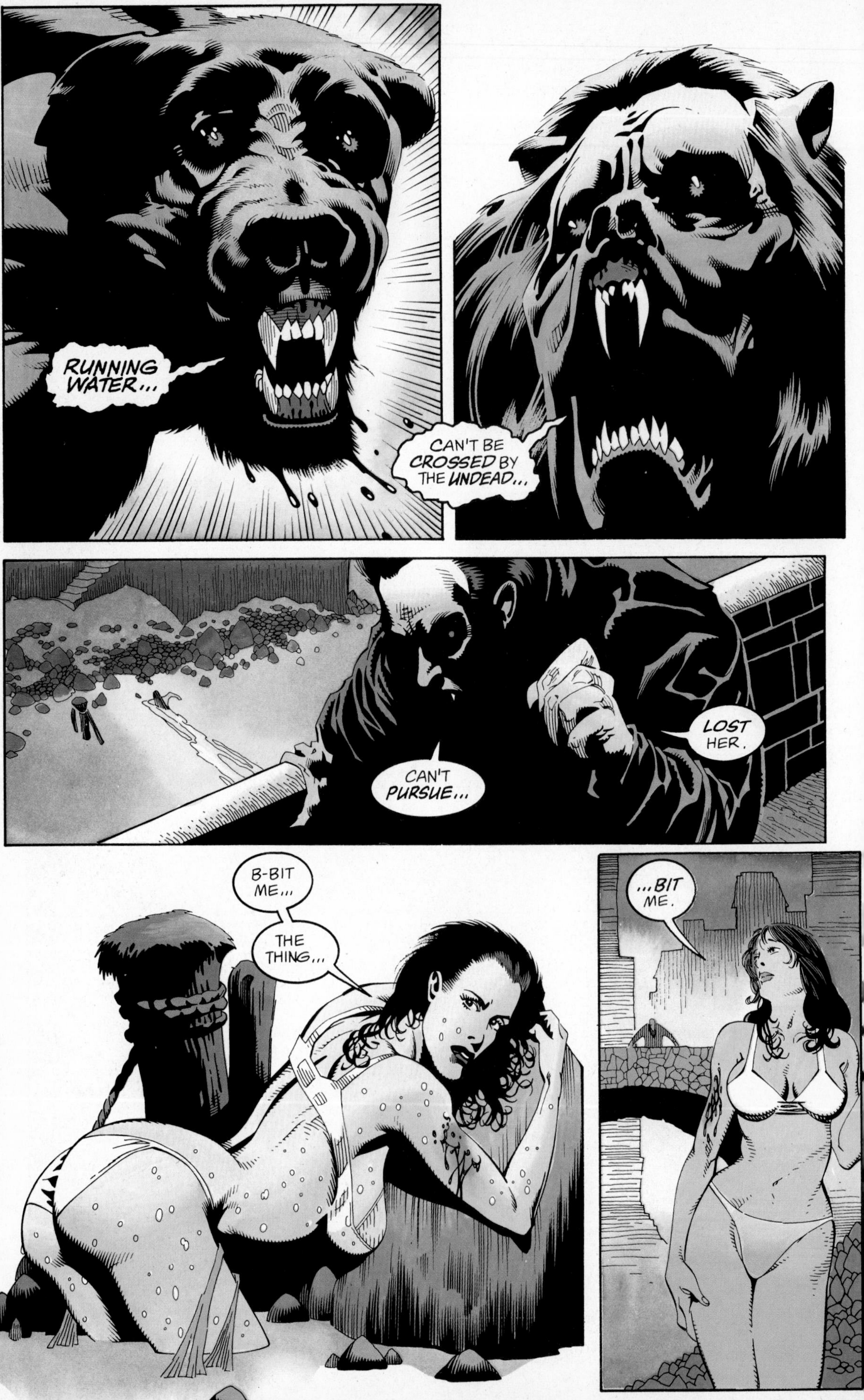

RUNNING WATER...
CAN'T BE CROSSED BY THE UNDEAD...
LOST HER.
CAN'T PURSUE...
B-BIT ME...
THE THING...
...BIT ME.

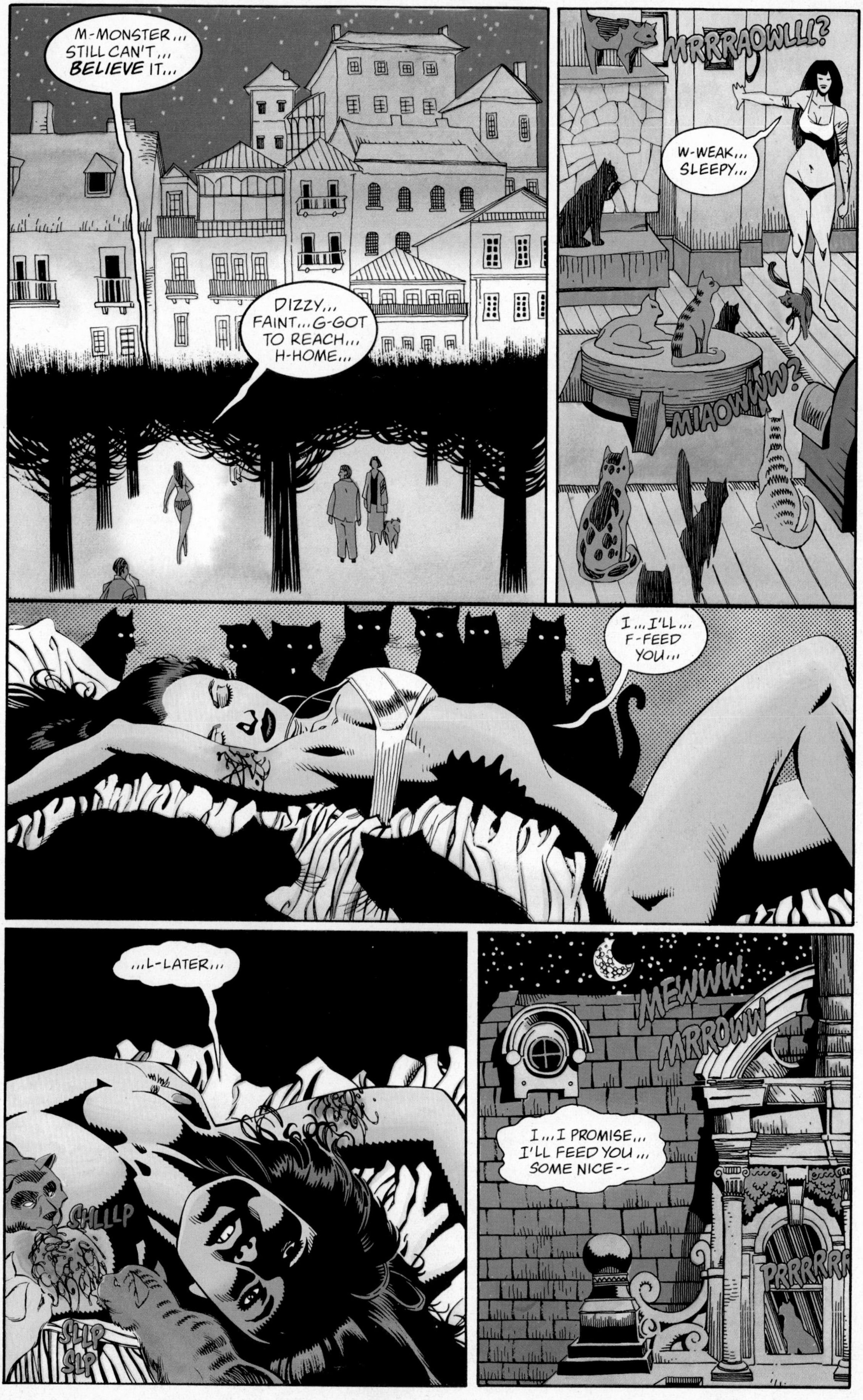
M-MONSTER... STILL CAN'T... BELIEVE IT...
DIZZY... FAINT...G-GOT TO REACH... H-HOME...
MRRRAOWLLL?
W-WEAK... SLEEPY...
MIAOWWW?
I...I'LL... F-FEED YOU...
...L-LATER...
SHLLLP
SLLP
SLP
MEWWW
MRROWW
I...I PROMISE... I'LL FEED YOU... SOME NICE--
PRRRRRR

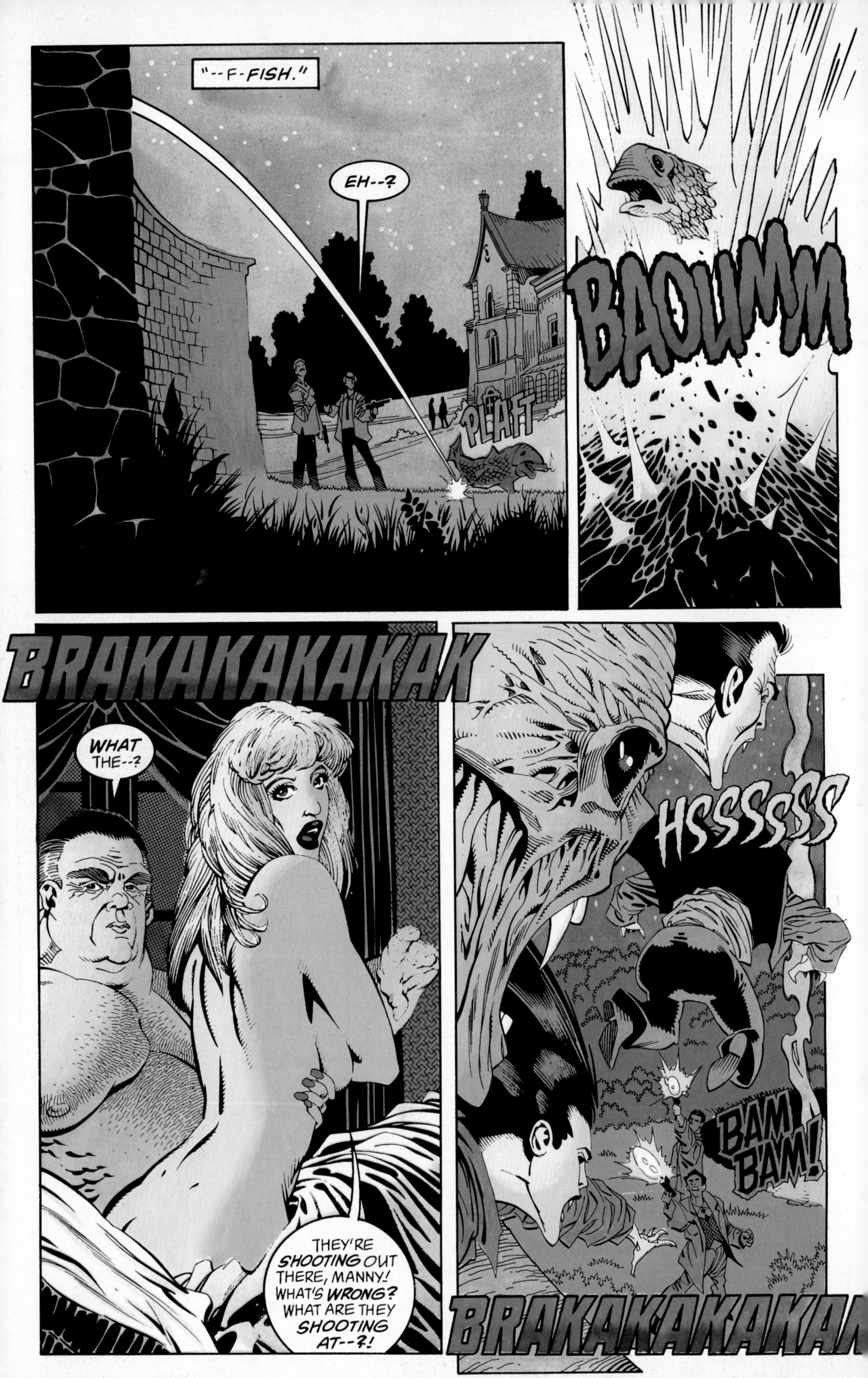
"--F-FISH."
EH--?
PLAFT
BAOUMM
BRAKAKAKAKAK
WHAT THE--?
THEY'RE SHOOTING OUT THERE, MANNY! WHAT'S WRONG? WHAT ARE THEY SHOOTING AT--?!
HSSSSSS
BAM BAM!
BRAKAKAKAKAKA

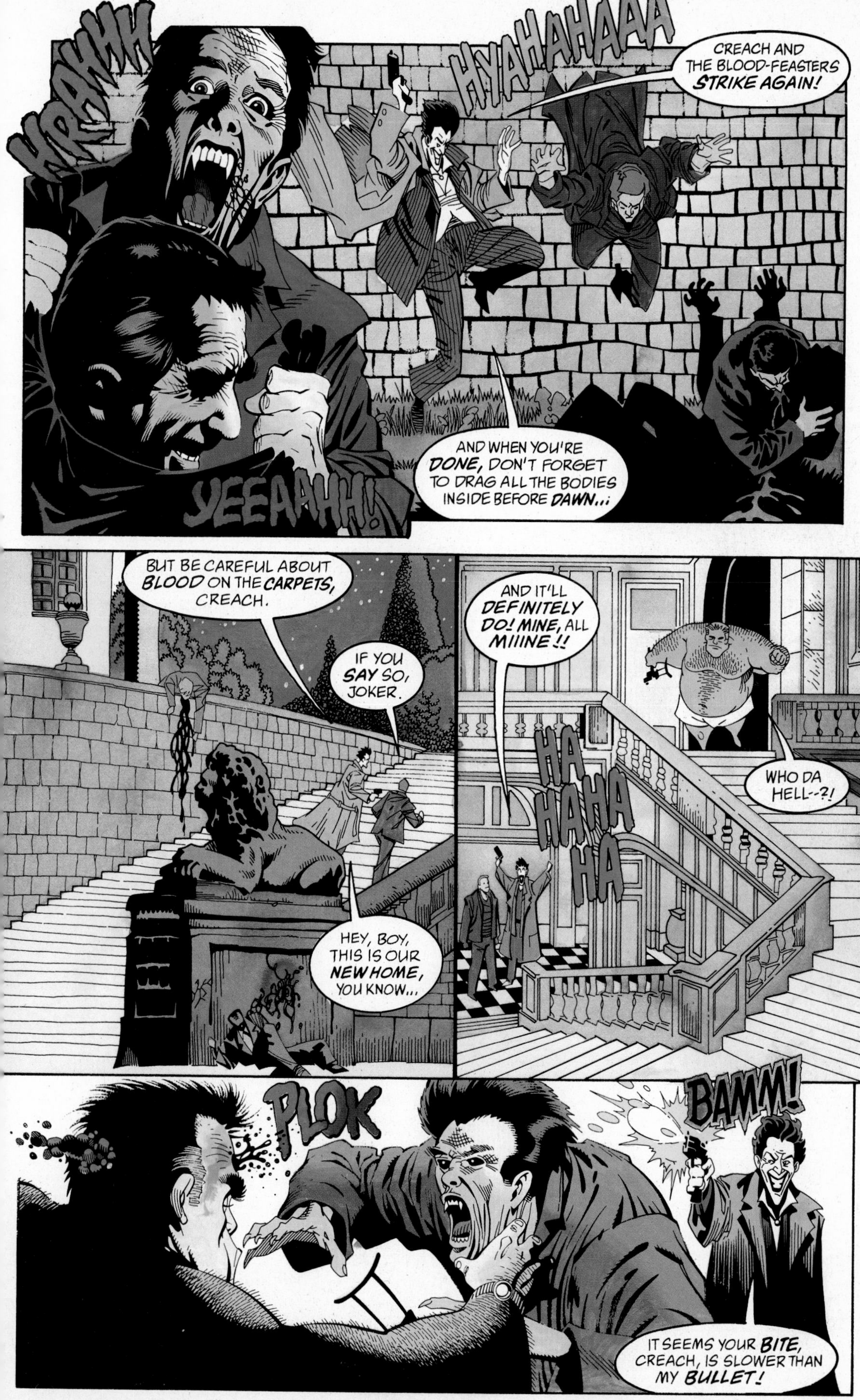
HRAHHH
HYAHAHAAA
CREACH AND THE BLOOD-FEASTERS STRIKE AGAIN!
AND WHEN YOU'RE DONE, DON'T FORGET TO DRAG ALL THE BODIES INSIDE BEFORE DAWN...
YEEAAHH!
BUT BE CAREFUL ABOUT BLOOD ON THE CARPETS, CREACH.
IF YOU SAY SO, JOKER.
HEY, BOY, THIS IS OUR NEW HOME, YOU KNOW...
AND IT'LL DEFINITELY DO! MINE, ALL MIIINE!!
HA HAHA HAHA HA
WHO DA HELL--?!
PLOK
BAMM!
IT SEEMS YOUR BITE, CREACH, IS SLOWER THAN MY BULLET!

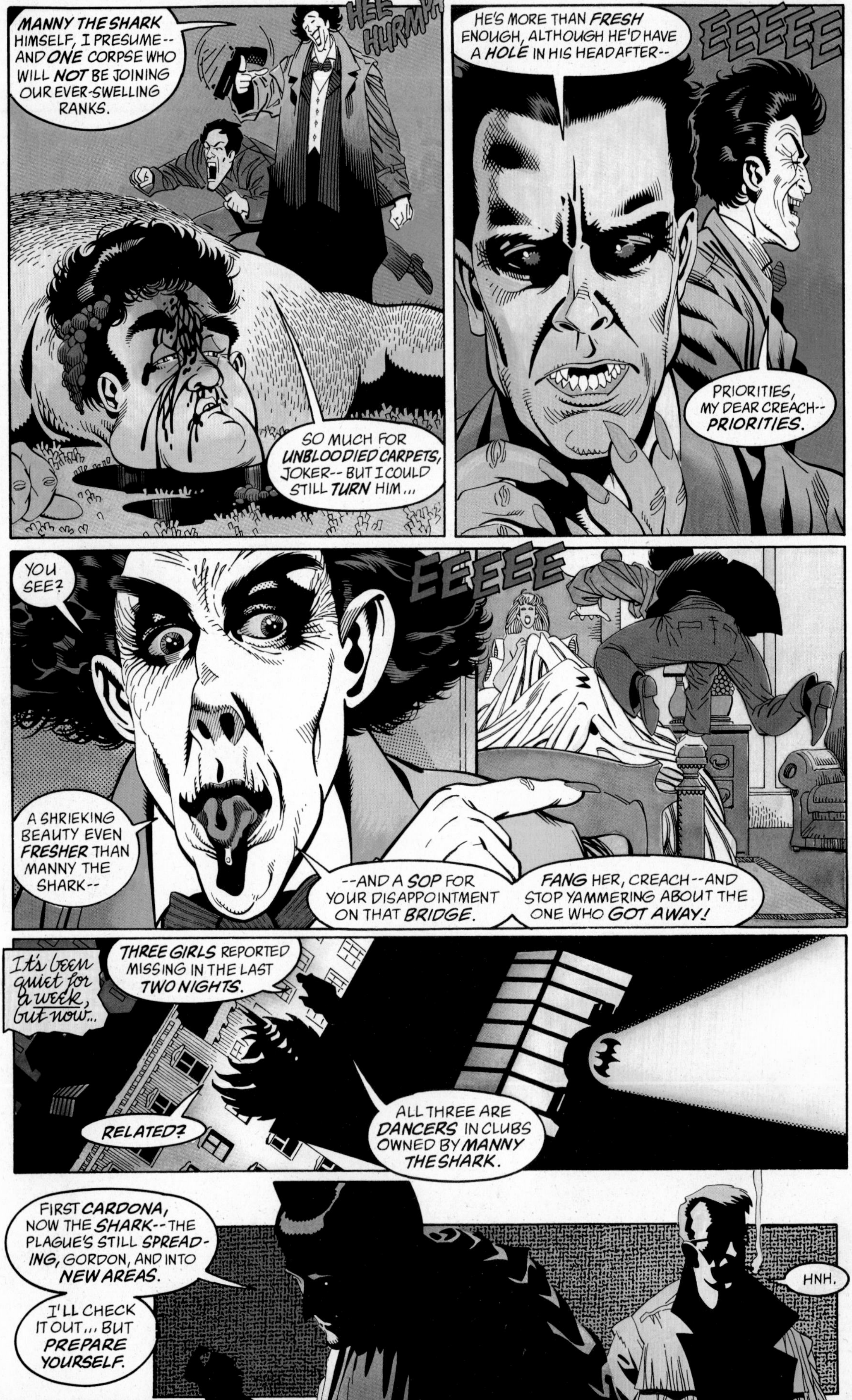
MANNY THE SHARK HIMSELF, I PRESUME-- AND ONE CORPSE WHO WILL NOT BE JOINING OUR EVER-SWELLING RANKS.
HEE HURMPH
SO MUCH FOR UNBLOODIED CARPETS, JOKER-- BUT I COULD STILL TURN HIM...
HE'S MORE THAN FRESH ENOUGH, ALTHOUGH HE'D HAVE A HOLE IN HIS HEAD AFTER--
EEEEE
PRIORITIES, MY DEAR CREACH-- PRIORITIES.
YOU SEE?
EEEEE
A SHRIEKING BEAUTY EVEN FRESHER THAN MANNY THE SHARK--
--AND A SOP FOR YOUR DISAPPOINTMENT ON THAT BRIDGE.
FANG HER, CREACH--AND STOP YAMMERING ABOUT THE ONE WHO GOT AWAY!
It's been quiet for a week, but now...
THREE GIRLS REPORTED MISSING IN THE LAST TWO NIGHTS.
RELATED?
ALL THREE ARE DANCERS IN CLUBS OWNED BY MANNY THE SHARK.
FIRST CARDONA, NOW THE SHARK-- THE PLAGUE'S STILL SPREAD-ING, GORDON, AND INTO NEW AREAS.
HNH.
I'LL CHECK IT OUT... BUT PREPARE YOURSELF.

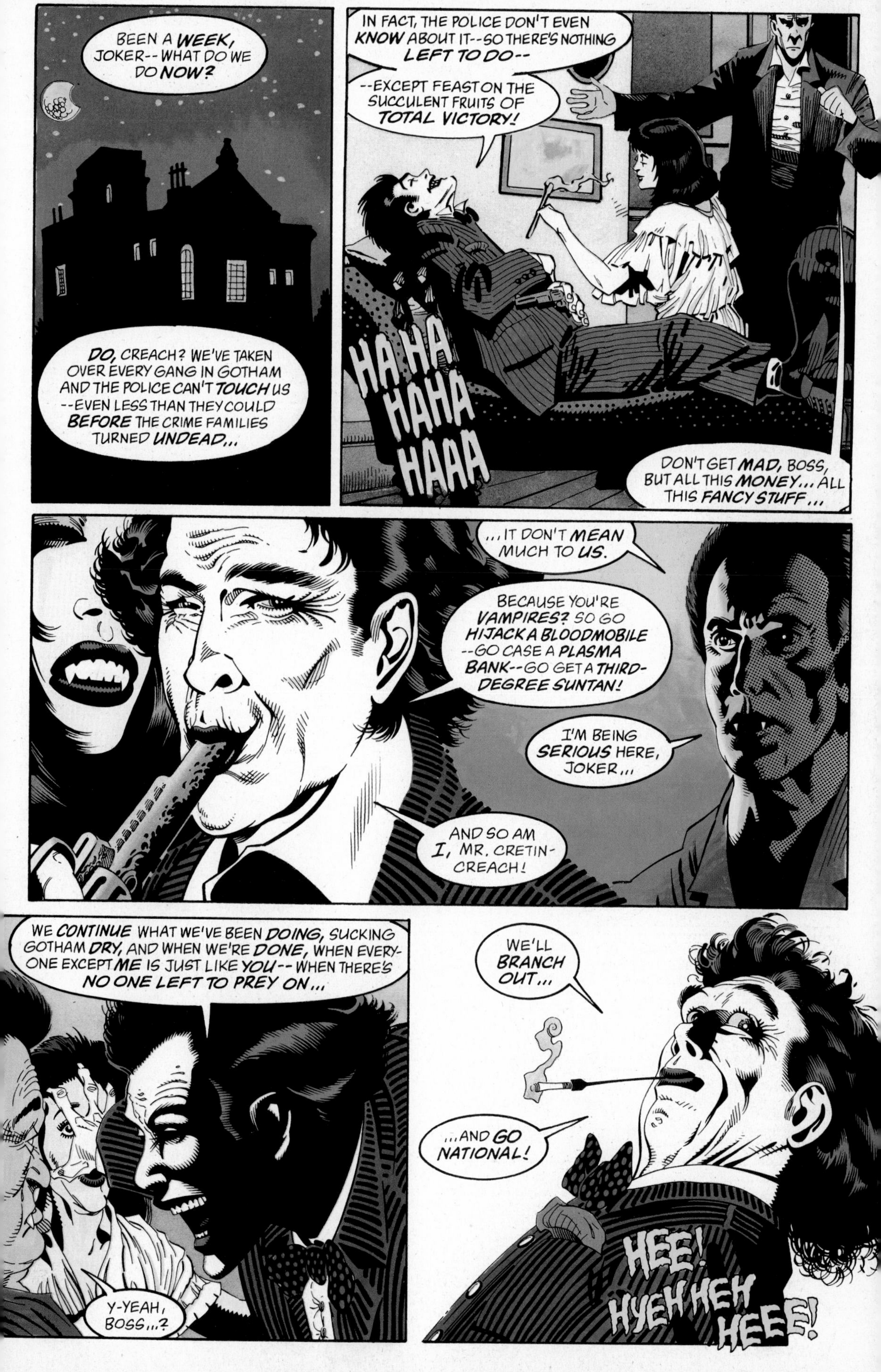
BEEN A WEEK, JOKER-- WHAT DO WE DO NOW?
DO, CREACH? WE'VE TAKEN OVER EVERY GANG IN GOTHAM AND THE POLICE CAN'T TOUCH US --EVEN LESS THAN THEY COULD BEFORE THE CRIME FAMILIES TURNED UNDEAD...
IN FACT, THE POLICE DON'T EVEN KNOW ABOUT IT--SO THERE'S NOTHING LEFT TO DO--
--EXCEPT FEAST ON THE SUCCULENT FRUITS OF TOTAL VICTORY!
HA HA HAHA HAAA
DON'T GET MAD, BOSS, BUT ALL THIS MONEY... ALL THIS FANCY STUFF...
...IT DON'T MEAN MUCH TO US.
BECAUSE YOU'RE VAMPIRES? SO GO HIJACK A BLOODMOBILE --GO CASE A PLASMA BANK--GO GET A THIRD-DEGREE SUNTAN!
I'M BEING SERIOUS HERE, JOKER...
AND SO AM I, MR. CRETIN-CREACH!
WE CONTINUE WHAT WE'VE BEEN DOING, SUCKING GOTHAM DRY, AND WHEN WE'RE DONE, WHEN EVERY-ONE EXCEPT ME IS JUST LIKE YOU-- WHEN THERE'S NO ONE LEFT TO PREY ON...
Y-YEAH, BOSS...?
WE'LL BRANCH OUT...
...AND GO NATIONAL!
HEE! HYEH HEH HEEE!

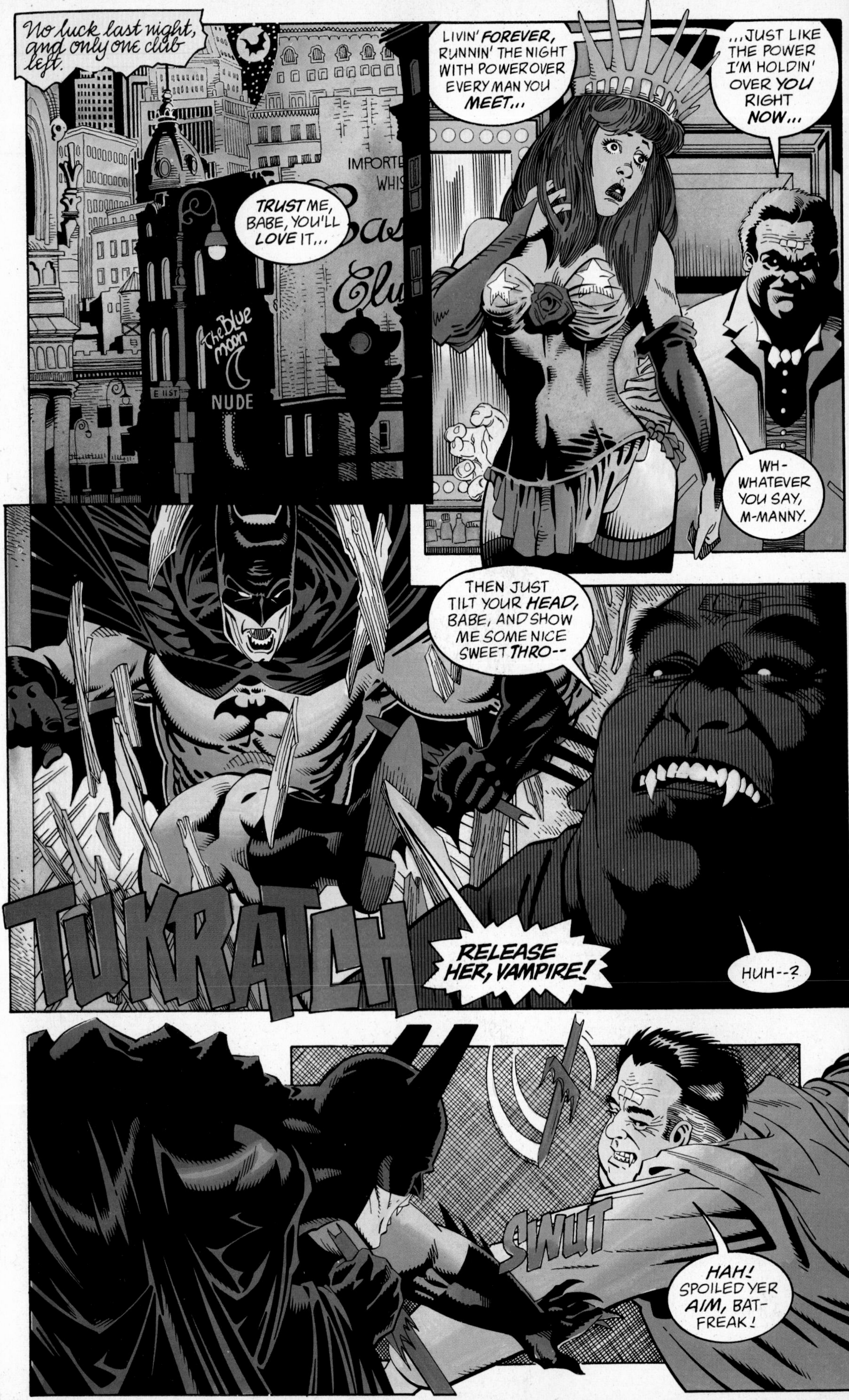

No luck last night, and only one club left.
TRUST ME, BABE, YOU'LL LOVE IT...
IMPORTE
WHIS
The Blue moon
NUDE
LIVIN' FOREVER, RUNNIN' THE NIGHT WITH POWER OVER EVERY MAN YOU MEET...
...JUST LIKE THE POWER I'M HOLDIN' OVER YOU RIGHT NOW...
WH-WHATEVER YOU SAY, M-MANNY.
THEN JUST TILT YOUR HEAD, BABE, AND SHOW ME SOME NICE SWEET THRO--
TUKRATCH
RELEASE HER, VAMPIRE!
HUH--?
SWUT
HAH! SPOILED YER AIM, BAT-FREAK!

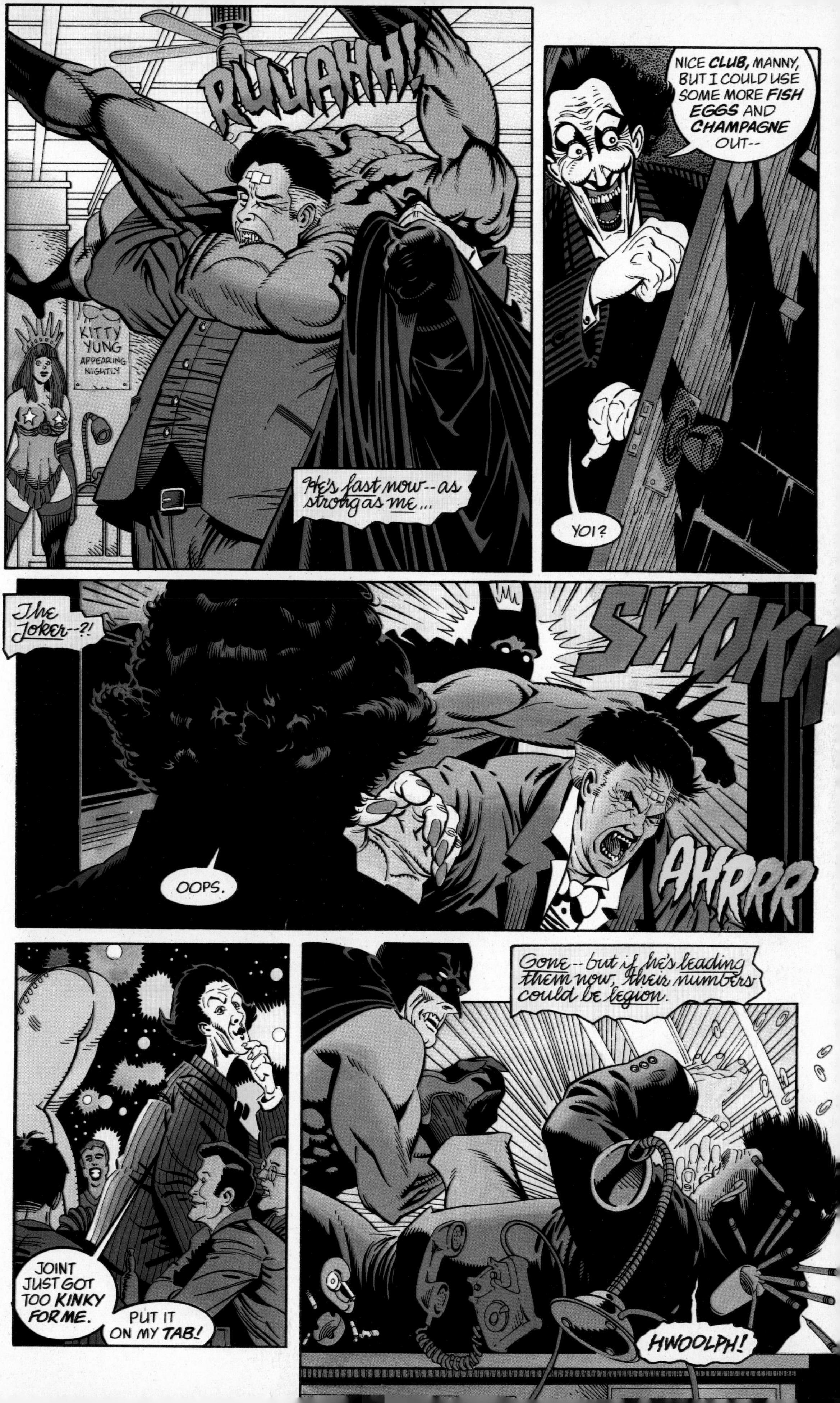
RUUAHH!
He's fast now--as strong as me...
NICE CLUB, MANNY, BUT I COULD USE SOME MORE FISH EGGS AND CHAMPAGNE OUT--
YOI?
The Joker--?!
SWOKK
OOPS.
AHRRR
JOINT JUST GOT TOO KINKY FOR ME.
PUT IT ON MY TAB!
Gone--but if he's leading them now, their numbers could be legion.
HWOOLPH!
KITTY YUNG APPEARING NIGHTLY

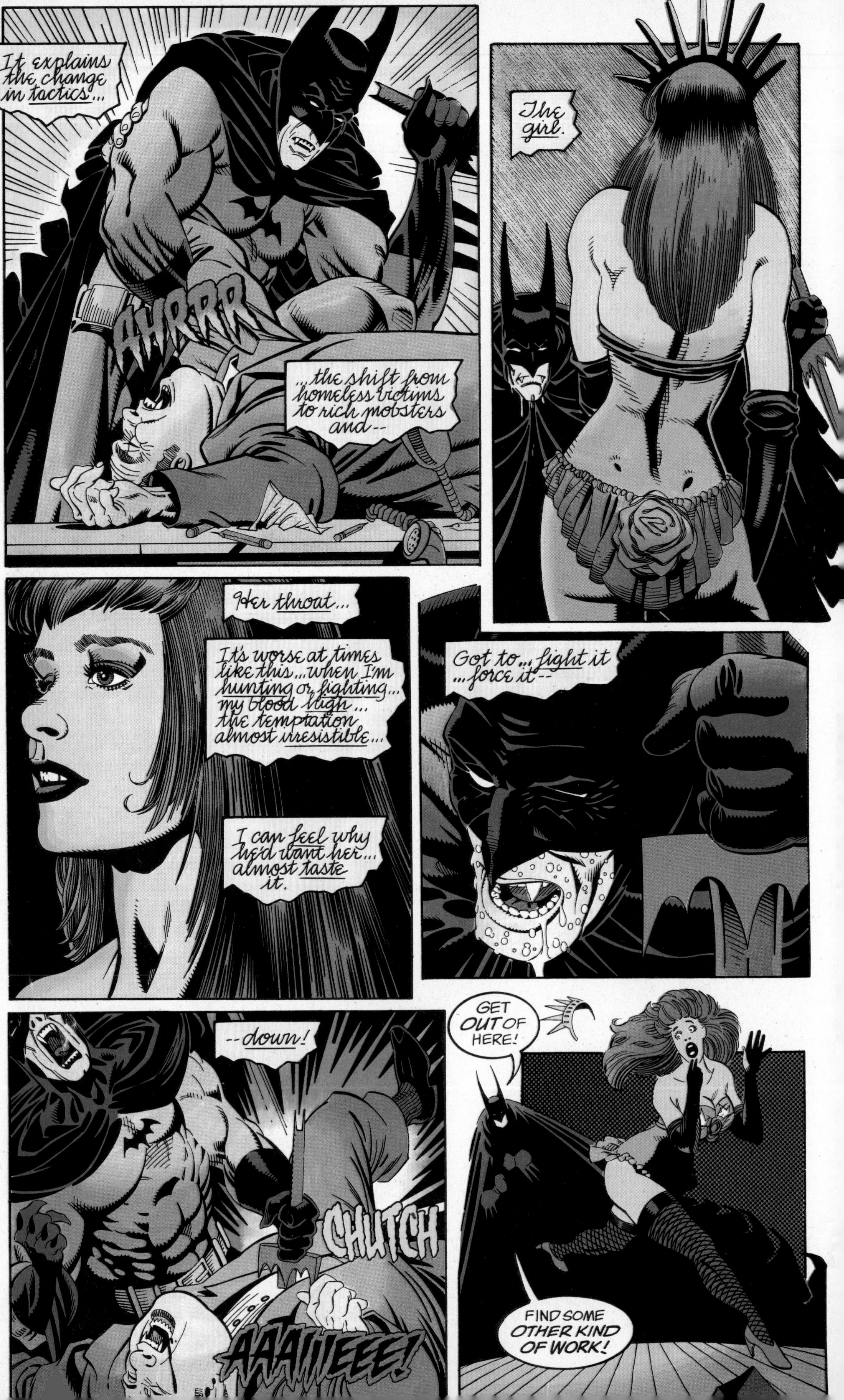

It explains the change in tactics...
AHRRR
...the shift from homeless victims to rich mobsters and--
The girl.
Her throat...
It's worse at times like this... when I'm hunting or fighting... my blood high... the temptation almost irresistible...
I can feel why he'd want her... almost taste it.
Got to... fight it ...force it--
--down!
CHUTCH
AAAIIIEEE!
GET OUT OF HERE!
FIND SOME OTHER KIND OF WORK!

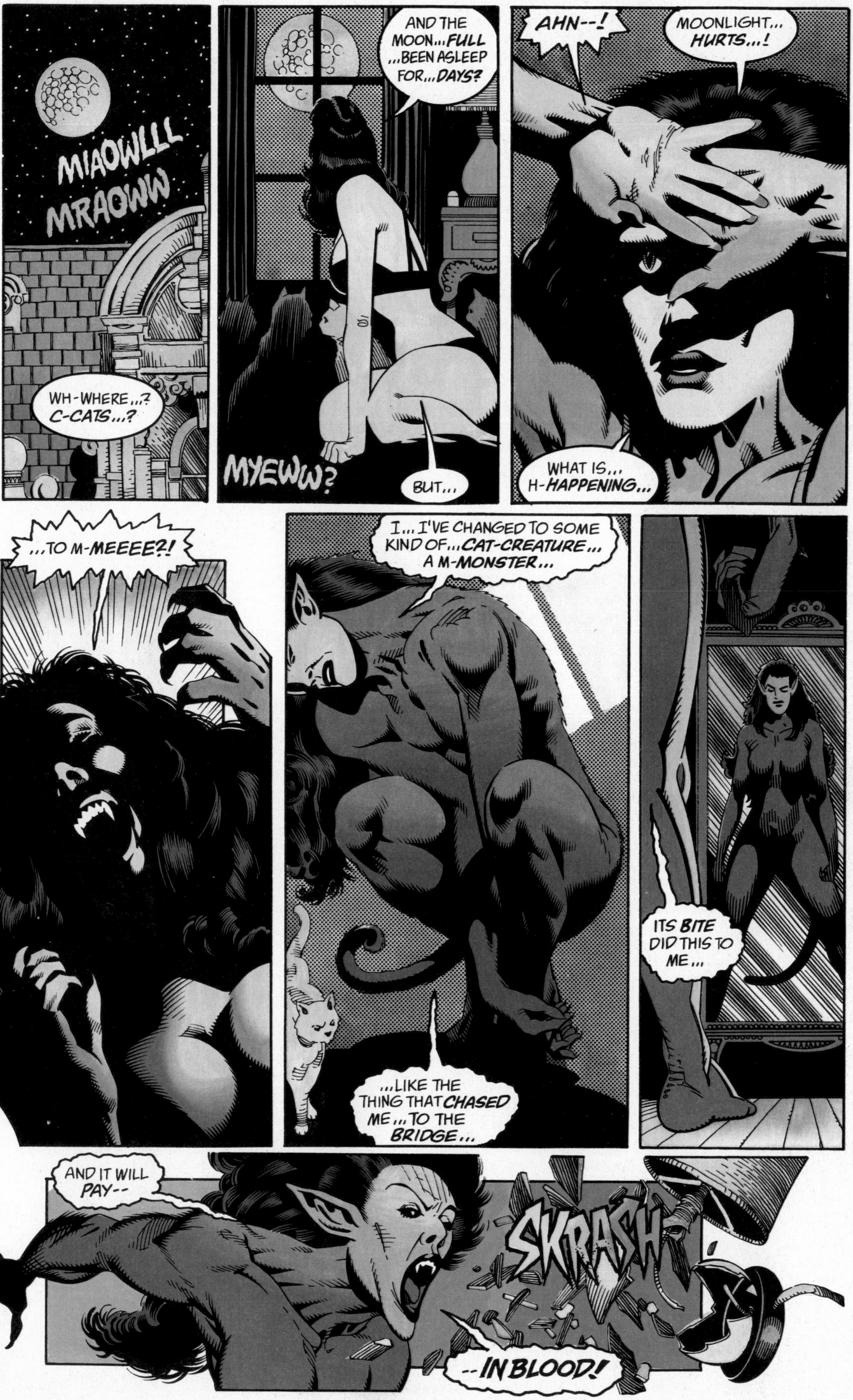
MIAOWLLL
MRAOWW
WH-WHERE...? C-CATS...?
AND THE MOON...FULL ...BEEN ASLEEP FOR...DAYS?
MYEWW?
BUT...
AHN--!
MOONLIGHT... HURTS...!
WHAT IS... H-HAPPENING...
...TO M-MEEEE?!
I... I'VE CHANGED TO SOME KIND OF...CAT-CREATURE... A M-MONSTER...
...LIKE THE THING THAT CHASED ME...TO THE BRIDGE...
ITS BITE DID THIS TO ME...
AND IT WILL PAY--
SKRASH
--IN BLOOD!

BAD NEWS, JOKER.

WE BEEN TAKIN' *HITS* THE LAST FEW NIGHTS.

BAD HITS-- A *LOT* OF THE FAMILY *DOWN.*

WILL RETURN TO **BLOOD-MANIA!!** AFTER THIS....

RCA

HITS--? HOW CAN YOU "HIT" A *VAMPIRE?*

WHO?

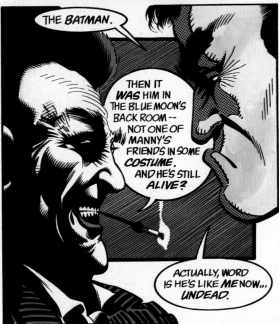

THE BATMAN.

THEN IT *WAS* HIM IN THE *BLUE MOON'S* BACK ROOM-- NOT ONE OF *MANNY'S* FRIENDS IN SOME *COSTUME.* AND HE'S STILL *ALIVE?*

ACTUALLY, WORD IS HE'S LIKE *ME* NOW... *UNDEAD.*

MIGHT HAVE *KNOWN--* THE MINUTE I GET INTO *VAMPIRES,* SO DOES *HE!* ALL THOSE STORIES ABOUT A "*BAT-MONSTER*" SWOOPING DOWN ON CRIMINALS ...

I WAS HOPING THEY WERE JUST *MISIDENTIFICATIONS* OF *OUR* PEOPLE.

SOME OF 'EM, MAYBE, BUT NOT *ALL.*

MANNY THE SHARK'S DEAD, AND SO'S *CARDONA--* FOR *GOOD* THIS TIME!

THE *BATMAN'S OUT* THERE, JOKER, AND HE'S *STAKIN'* US *DOWN!*

THEN WE'LL JUST HAVE TO TAKE *HIM* DOWN, WON'T WE, *CREACH?*

HEH HEH HEHRRR

SOME SORT OF *TRAP...*

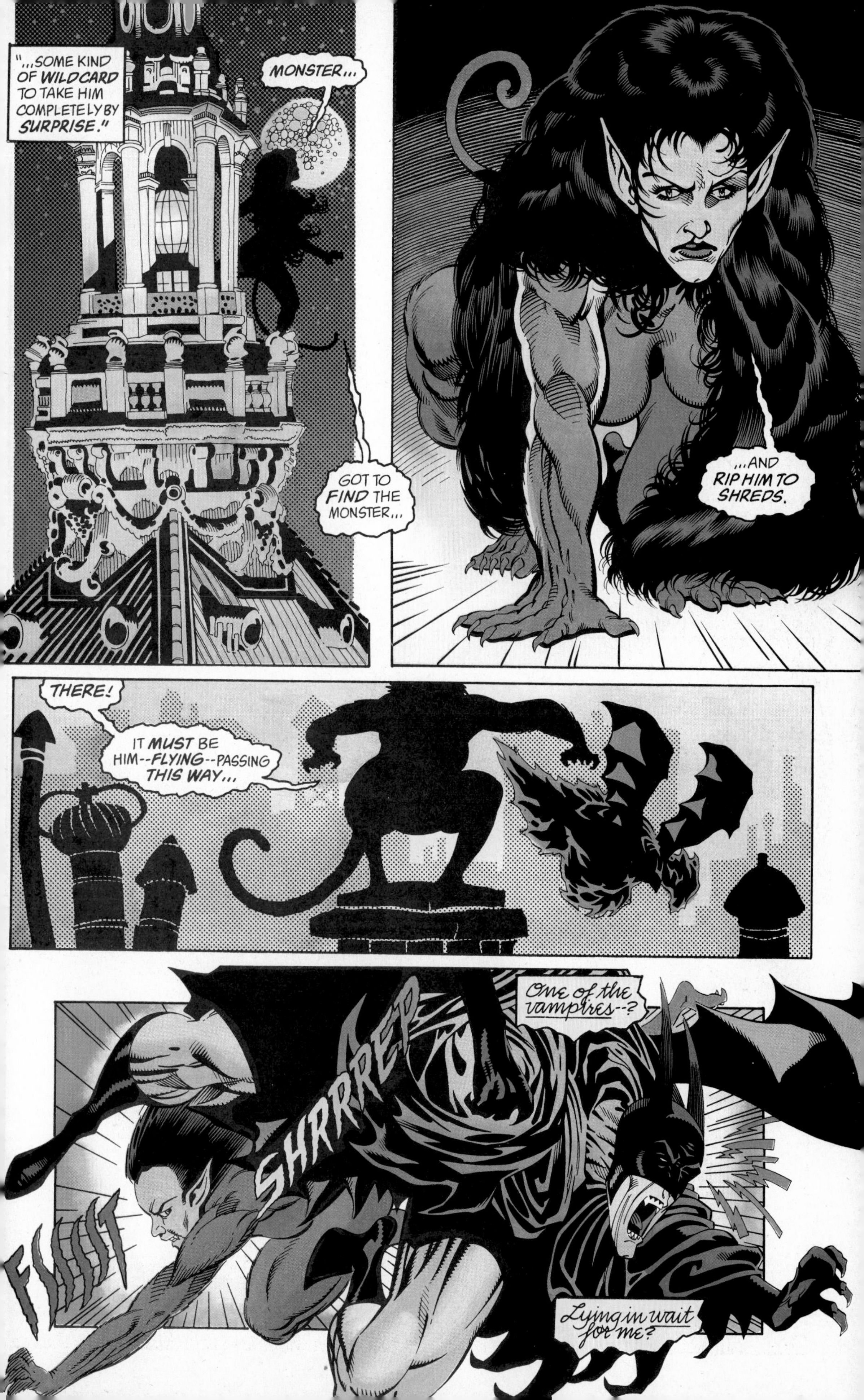
"...SOME KIND OF WILDCARD TO TAKE HIM COMPLETELY BY SURPRISE."
MONSTER...
GOT TO FIND THE MONSTER...
...AND RIP HIM TO SHREDS.
THERE!
IT MUST BE HIM--FLYING--PASSING THIS WAY...
One of the vampires--?
SHRRREP
FLUUT
Lying in wait for me?

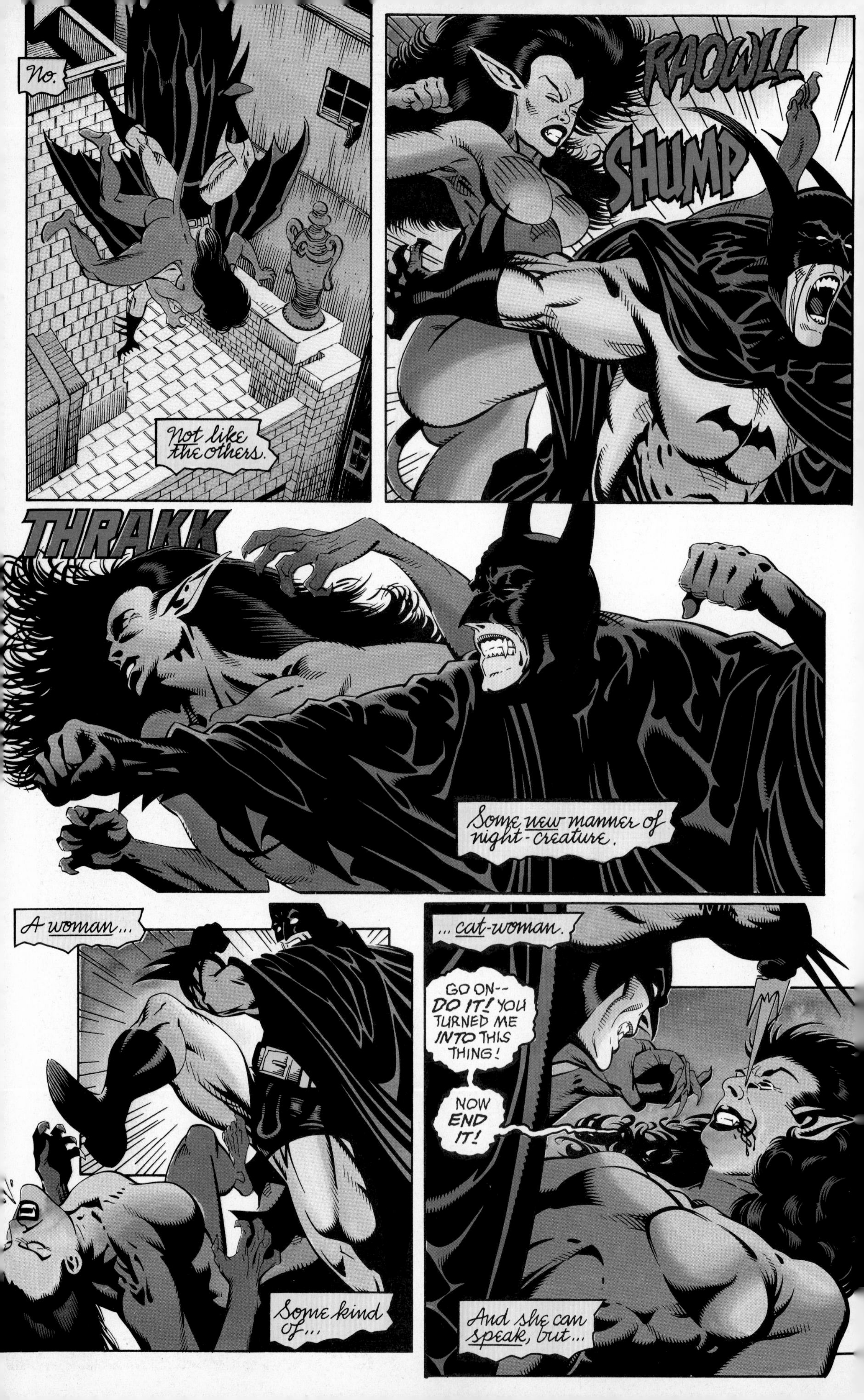
No.
Not like the others.
RAOWLL
SHUMP
THRAKK
Some new manner of night-creature.
A woman...
Some kind of...
...cat-woman.
GO ON-- DO IT! YOU TURNED ME INTO THIS THING!
NOW END IT!
And she can speak, but...

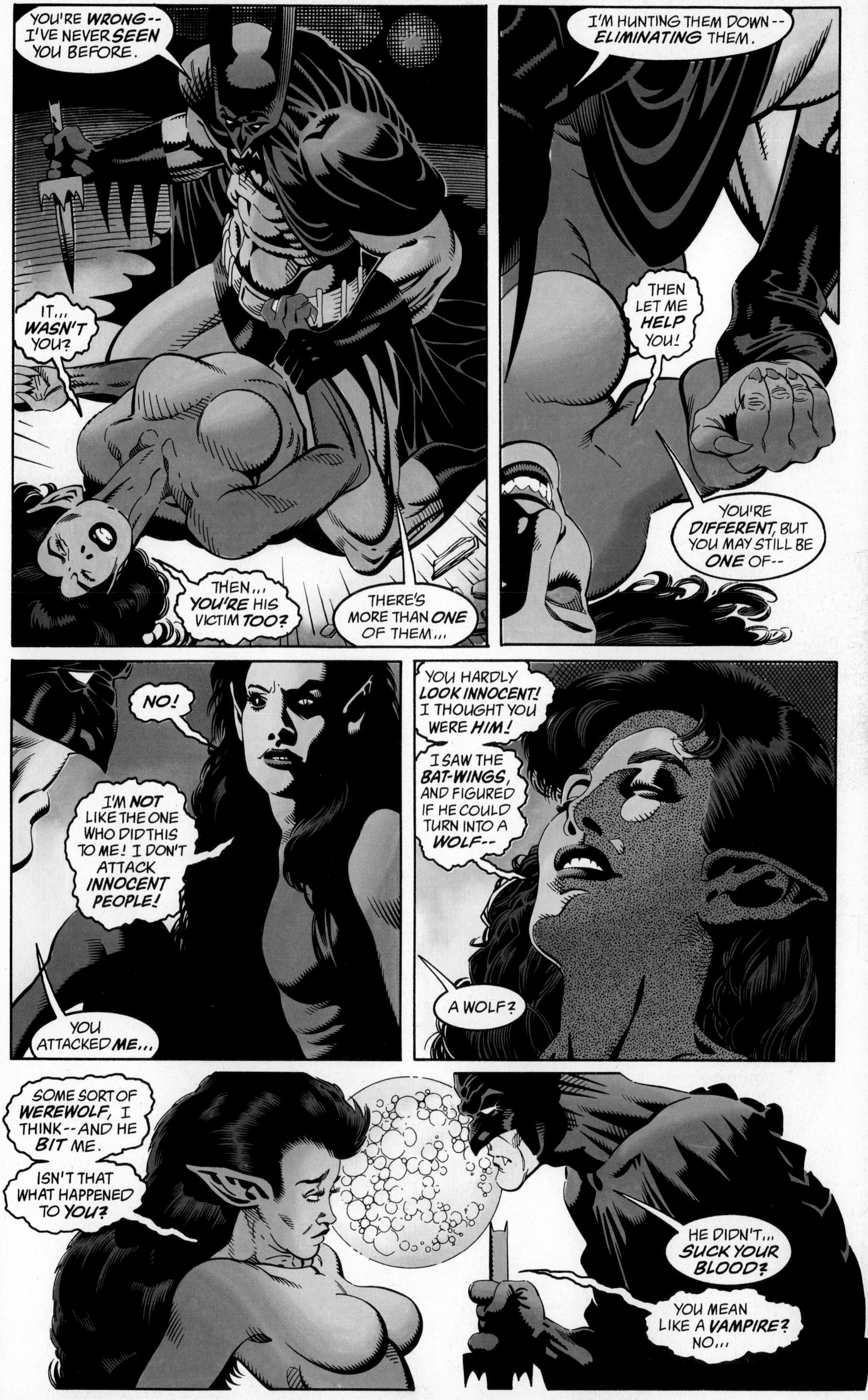
YOU'RE WRONG-- I'VE NEVER SEEN YOU BEFORE.
IT... WASN'T YOU?
THEN... YOU'RE HIS VICTIM TOO?
THERE'S MORE THAN ONE OF THEM...
I'M HUNTING THEM DOWN-- ELIMINATING THEM.
THEN LET ME HELP YOU!
YOU'RE DIFFERENT, BUT YOU MAY STILL BE ONE OF--
NO!
I'M NOT LIKE THE ONE WHO DID THIS TO ME! I DON'T ATTACK INNOCENT PEOPLE!
YOU ATTACKED ME...
YOU HARDLY LOOK INNOCENT! I THOUGHT YOU WERE HIM!
I SAW THE BAT-WINGS, AND FIGURED IF HE COULD TURN INTO A WOLF--
A WOLF?
SOME SORT OF WEREWOLF, I THINK--AND HE BIT ME.
ISN'T THAT WHAT HAPPENED TO YOU?
HE DIDN'T... SUCK YOUR BLOOD?
YOU MEAN LIKE A VAMPIRE? NO...

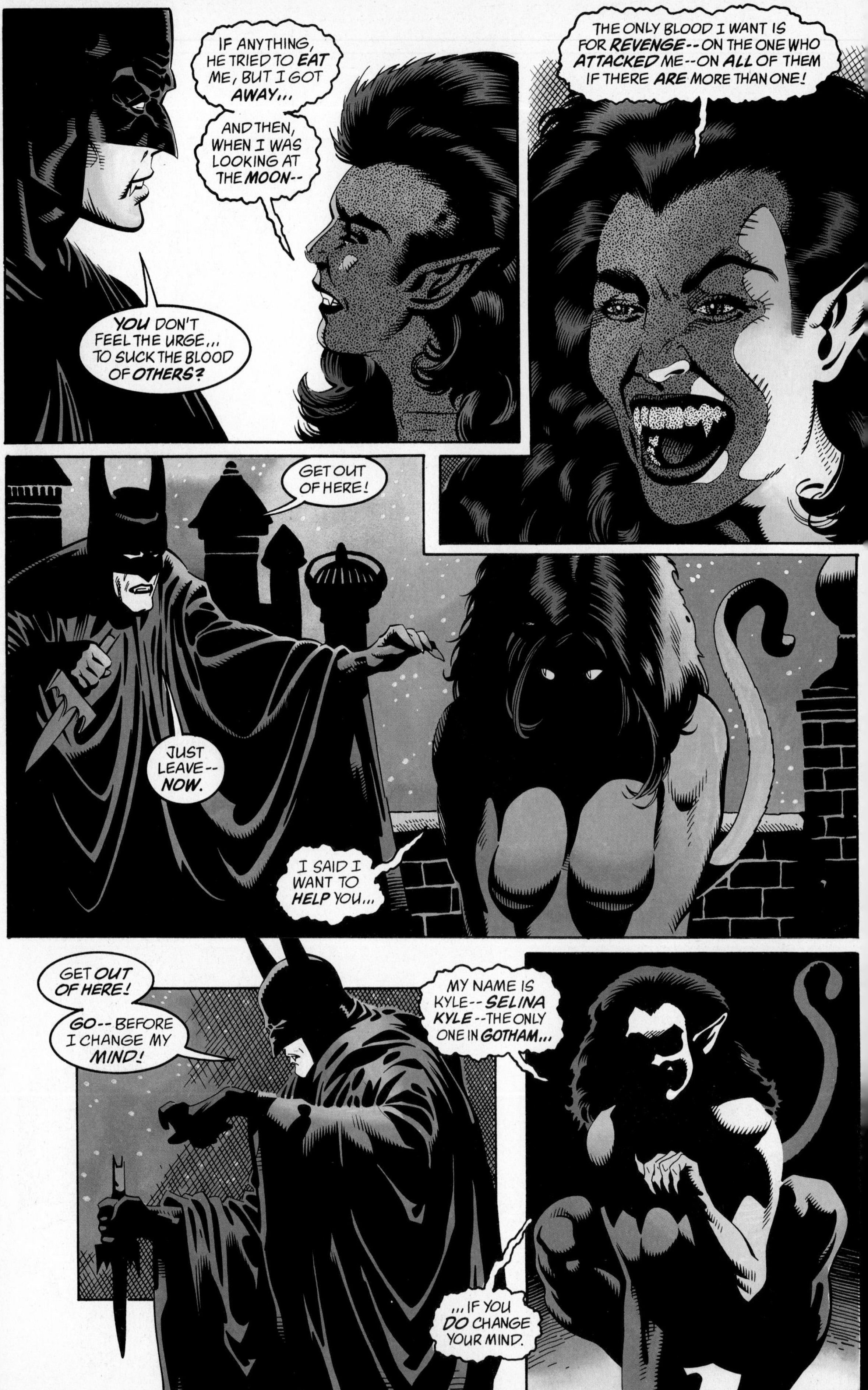
IF ANYTHING, HE TRIED TO EAT ME, BUT I GOT AWAY...
AND THEN, WHEN I WAS LOOKING AT THE MOON--
YOU DON'T FEEL THE URGE... TO SUCK THE BLOOD OF OTHERS?
THE ONLY BLOOD I WANT IS FOR REVENGE--ON THE ONE WHO ATTACKED ME--ON ALL OF THEM IF THERE ARE MORE THAN ONE!
GET OUT OF HERE!
JUST LEAVE-- NOW.
I SAID I WANT TO HELP YOU...
GET OUT OF HERE!
GO--BEFORE I CHANGE MY MIND!
MY NAME IS KYLE--SELINA KYLE--THE ONLY ONE IN GOTHAM...
...IF YOU DO CHANGE YOUR MIND.

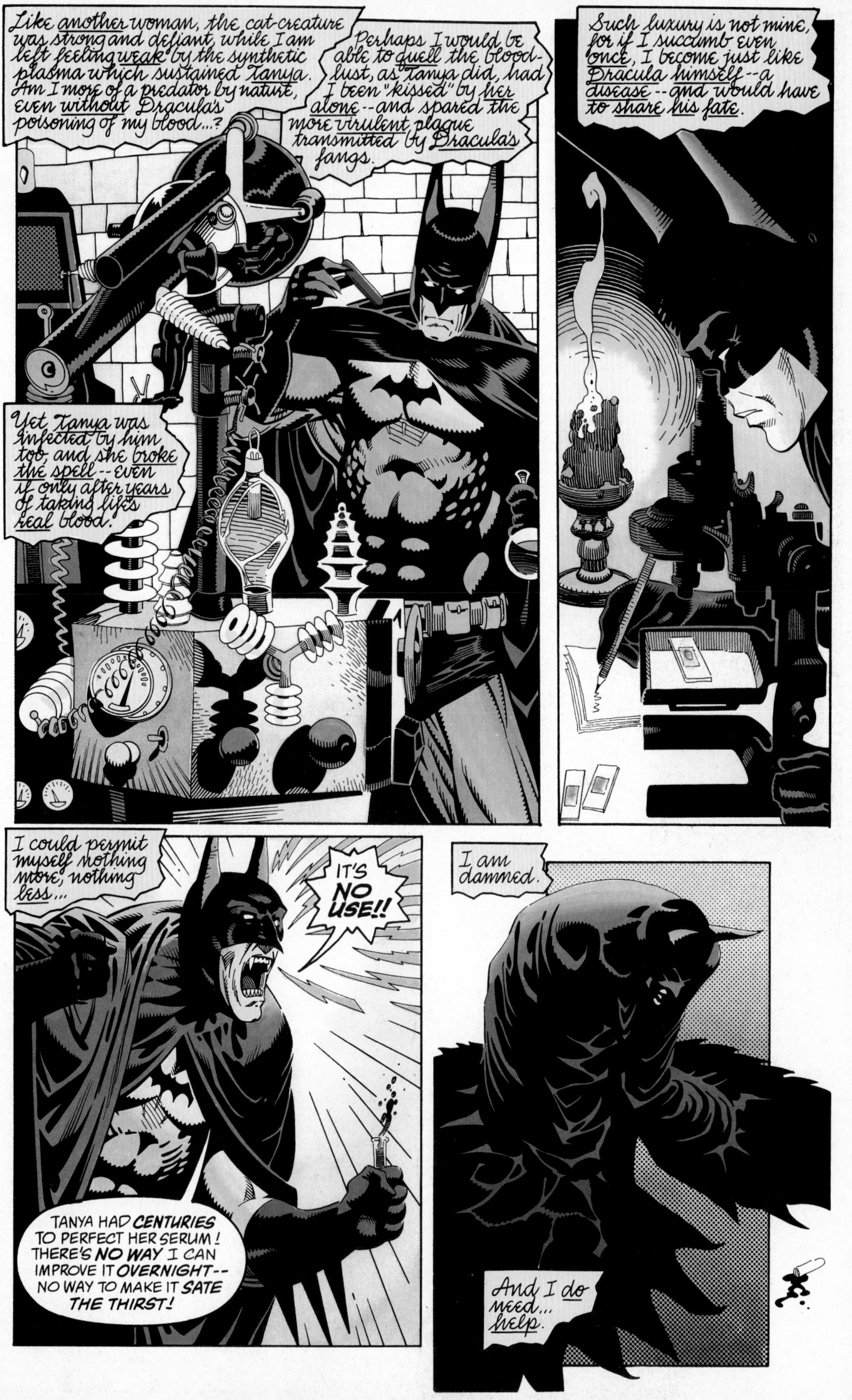
Like another woman, the cat-creature was strong and defiant, while I am left feeling weak by the synthetic plasma which sustained Tanya. Am I more of a predator by nature, even without Dracula's poisoning of my blood...?
Perhaps I would be able to quell the blood-lust, as Tanya did, had I been "kissed" by her alone--and spared the more virulent plague transmitted by Dracula's fangs.
Yet Tanya was infected by him too, and she broke the spell--even if only after years of taking life's real blood.
Such luxury is not mine, for if I succumb even once, I become just like Dracula himself--a disease--and would have to share his fate.
I could permit myself nothing more, nothing less...
IT'S NO USE!!
TANYA HAD CENTURIES TO PERFECT HER SERUM! THERE'S NO WAY I CAN IMPROVE IT OVERNIGHT--NO WAY TO MAKE IT SATE THE THIRST!
I am damned.
And I do need... help.

ARIANE... TELL ME ABOUT... WERE-CREATURES.

I KNEW I FELT THAT DRAFT AGAIN...

... AND I ASSUME YOU'RE REFERRING TO THOSE SAID TO TAKE THE FORM OF THEIR ANIMAL "TOTEM," USUALLY A WOLF.

BUT NOT ALWAYS A WOLF?

INDEED NOT.

VAMPIRES SUPPOSEDLY TRANSFORM INTO BATS-- AND IN INDIA, FOR EXAMPLE, WERE-TIGERS ARE MOST PREVALENT.

WERE-CATS...

YES, WHILE OTHER CULTURES FAVOR OTHER CREATURES -- WERE-APES, BEARS, CROCODILES, RIGHT THROUGH THE ENTIRE BESTIARY OF PREDATORS.

AND MUST THESE WERE-CREATURES BE EVIL?

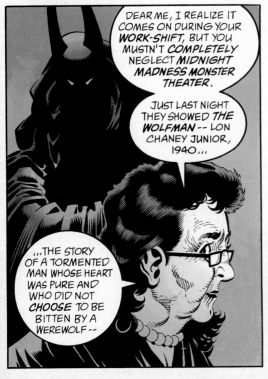

DEAR ME, I REALIZE IT COMES ON DURING YOUR WORK-SHIFT, BUT YOU MUSTN'T COMPLETELY NEGLECT MIDNIGHT MADNESS MONSTER THEATER.

JUST LAST NIGHT THEY SHOWED THE WOLFMAN -- LON CHANEY JUNIOR, 1940...

...THE STORY OF A TORMENTED MAN WHOSE HEART WAS PURE AND WHO DID NOT CHOOSE TO BE BITTEN BY A WEREWOLF --

--BUT WHO NEVERTHELESS BECAME A WOLF-CREATURE HIMSELF --

--"WHEN THE WOLFBANE BLOOMED AND THE MOON WAS FULL."

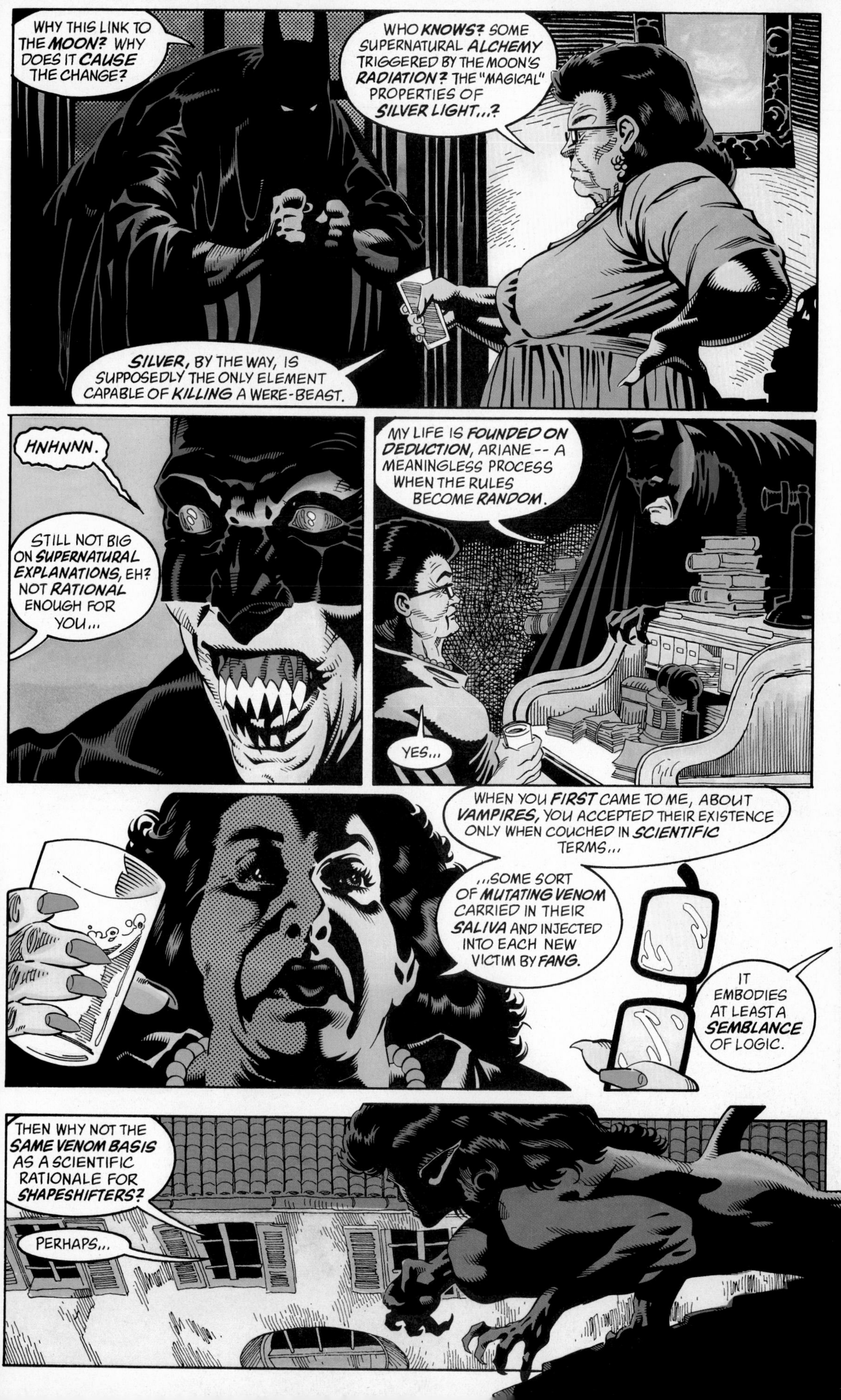
WHY THIS LINK TO THE MOON? WHY DOES IT CAUSE THE CHANGE?
WHO KNOWS? SOME SUPERNATURAL ALCHEMY TRIGGERED BY THE MOON'S RADIATION? THE "MAGICAL" PROPERTIES OF SILVER LIGHT...?
SILVER, BY THE WAY, IS SUPPOSEDLY THE ONLY ELEMENT CAPABLE OF KILLING A WERE-BEAST.
HNHNNN.
STILL NOT BIG ON SUPERNATURAL EXPLANATIONS, EH? NOT RATIONAL ENOUGH FOR YOU...
MY LIFE IS FOUNDED ON DEDUCTION, ARIANE -- A MEANINGLESS PROCESS WHEN THE RULES BECOME RANDOM.
YES...
WHEN YOU FIRST CAME TO ME, ABOUT VAMPIRES, YOU ACCEPTED THEIR EXISTENCE ONLY WHEN COUCHED IN SCIENTIFIC TERMS...
...SOME SORT OF MUTATING VENOM CARRIED IN THEIR SALIVA AND INJECTED INTO EACH NEW VICTIM BY FANG.
IT EMBODIES AT LEAST A SEMBLANCE OF LOGIC.
THEN WHY NOT THE SAME VENOM BASIS AS A SCIENTIFIC RATIONALE FOR SHAPESHIFTERS?
PERHAPS...

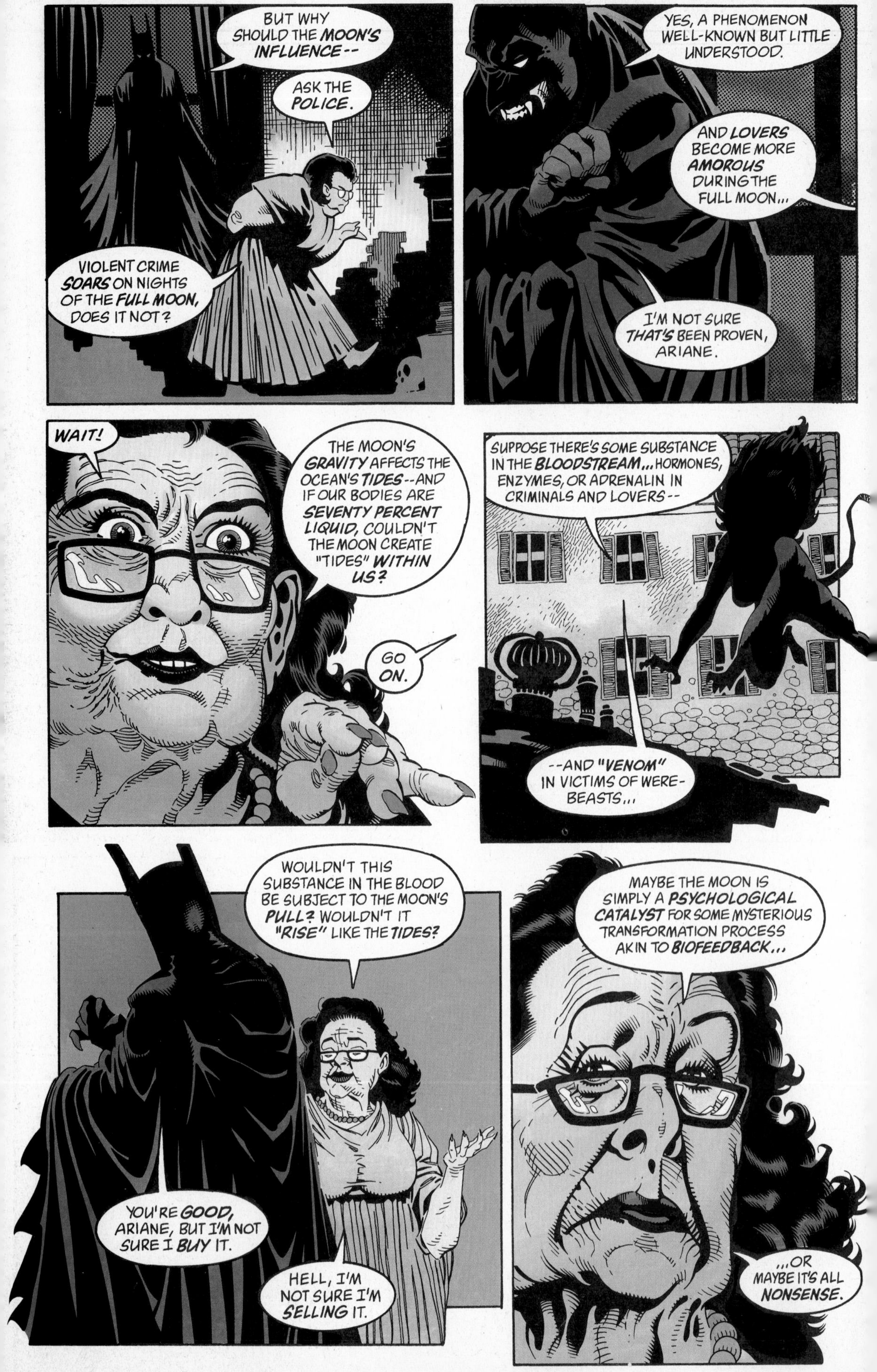
BUT WHY SHOULD THE MOON'S INFLUENCE--
ASK THE POLICE.
VIOLENT CRIME SOARS ON NIGHTS OF THE FULL MOON, DOES IT NOT?
YES, A PHENOMENON WELL-KNOWN BUT LITTLE UNDERSTOOD.
AND LOVERS BECOME MORE AMOROUS DURING THE FULL MOON...
I'M NOT SURE THAT'S BEEN PROVEN, ARIANE.
WAIT!
THE MOON'S GRAVITY AFFECTS THE OCEAN'S TIDES--AND IF OUR BODIES ARE SEVENTY PERCENT LIQUID, COULDN'T THE MOON CREATE "TIDES" WITHIN US?
GO ON.
SUPPOSE THERE'S SOME SUBSTANCE IN THE BLOODSTREAM... HORMONES, ENZYMES, OR ADRENALIN IN CRIMINALS AND LOVERS--
--AND "VENOM" IN VICTIMS OF WERE-BEASTS...
WOULDN'T THIS SUBSTANCE IN THE BLOOD BE SUBJECT TO THE MOON'S PULL? WOULDN'T IT "RISE" LIKE THE TIDES?
YOU'RE GOOD, ARIANE, BUT I'M NOT SURE I BUY IT.
HELL, I'M NOT SURE I'M SELLING IT.
MAYBE THE MOON IS SIMPLY A PSYCHOLOGICAL CATALYST FOR SOME MYSTERIOUS TRANSFORMATION PROCESS AKIN TO BIOFEEDBACK...
...OR MAYBE IT'S ALL NONSENSE.

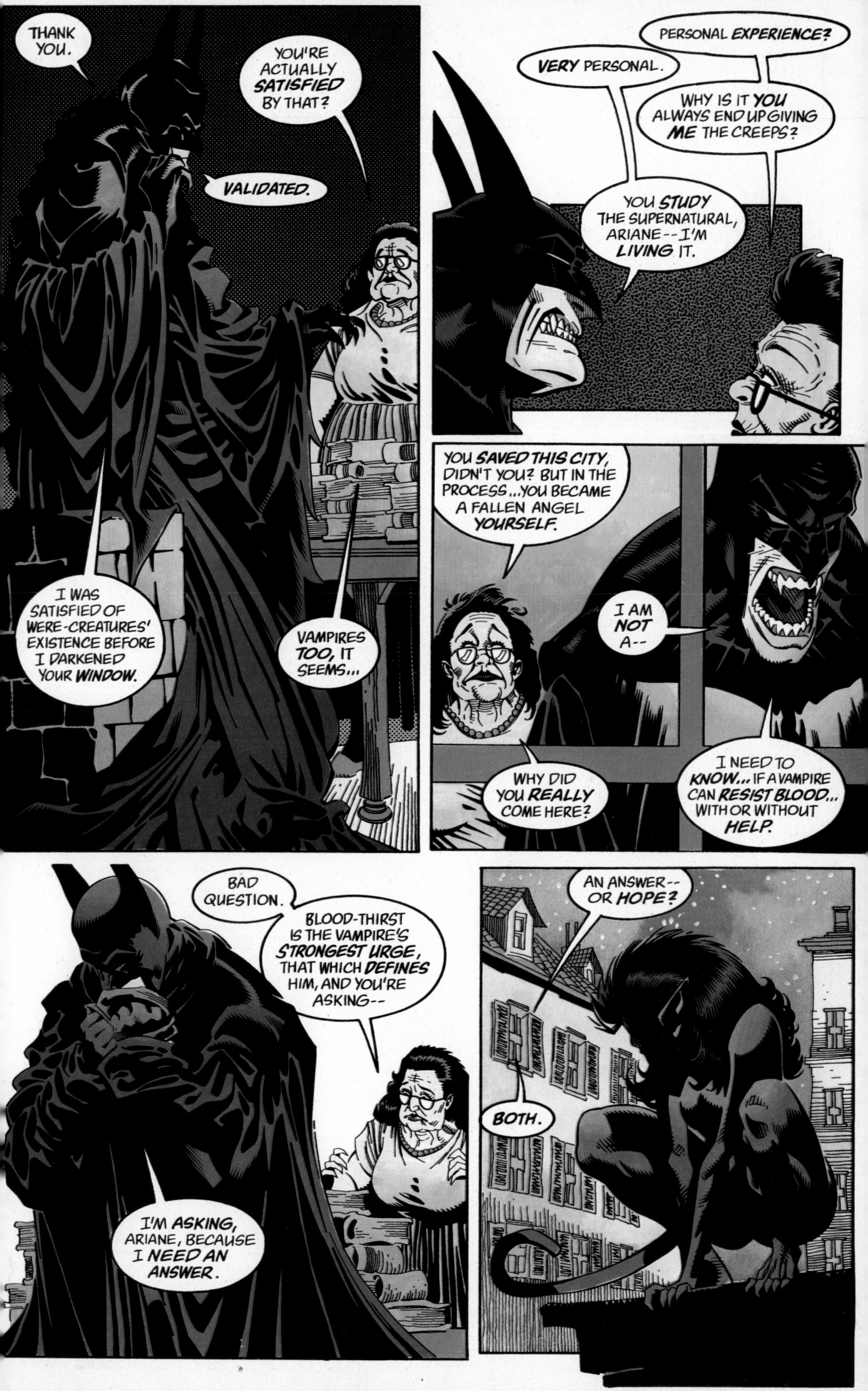
THANK YOU.
YOU'RE ACTUALLY SATISFIED BY THAT?
VALIDATED.
I WAS SATISFIED OF WERE-CREATURES' EXISTENCE BEFORE I DARKENED YOUR WINDOW.
VAMPIRES TOO, IT SEEMS...
PERSONAL EXPERIENCE?
VERY PERSONAL.
WHY IS IT YOU ALWAYS END UP GIVING ME THE CREEPS?
YOU STUDY THE SUPERNATURAL, ARIANE--I'M LIVING IT.
YOU SAVED THIS CITY, DIDN'T YOU? BUT IN THE PROCESS...YOU BECAME A FALLEN ANGEL YOURSELF.
I AM NOT A--
WHY DID YOU REALLY COME HERE?
I NEED TO KNOW... IF A VAMPIRE CAN RESIST BLOOD... WITH OR WITHOUT HELP.
BAD QUESTION.
BLOOD-THIRST IS THE VAMPIRE'S STRONGEST URGE, THAT WHICH DEFINES HIM, AND YOU'RE ASKING--
I'M ASKING, ARIANE, BECAUSE I NEED AN ANSWER.
AN ANSWER--OR HOPE?
BOTH.

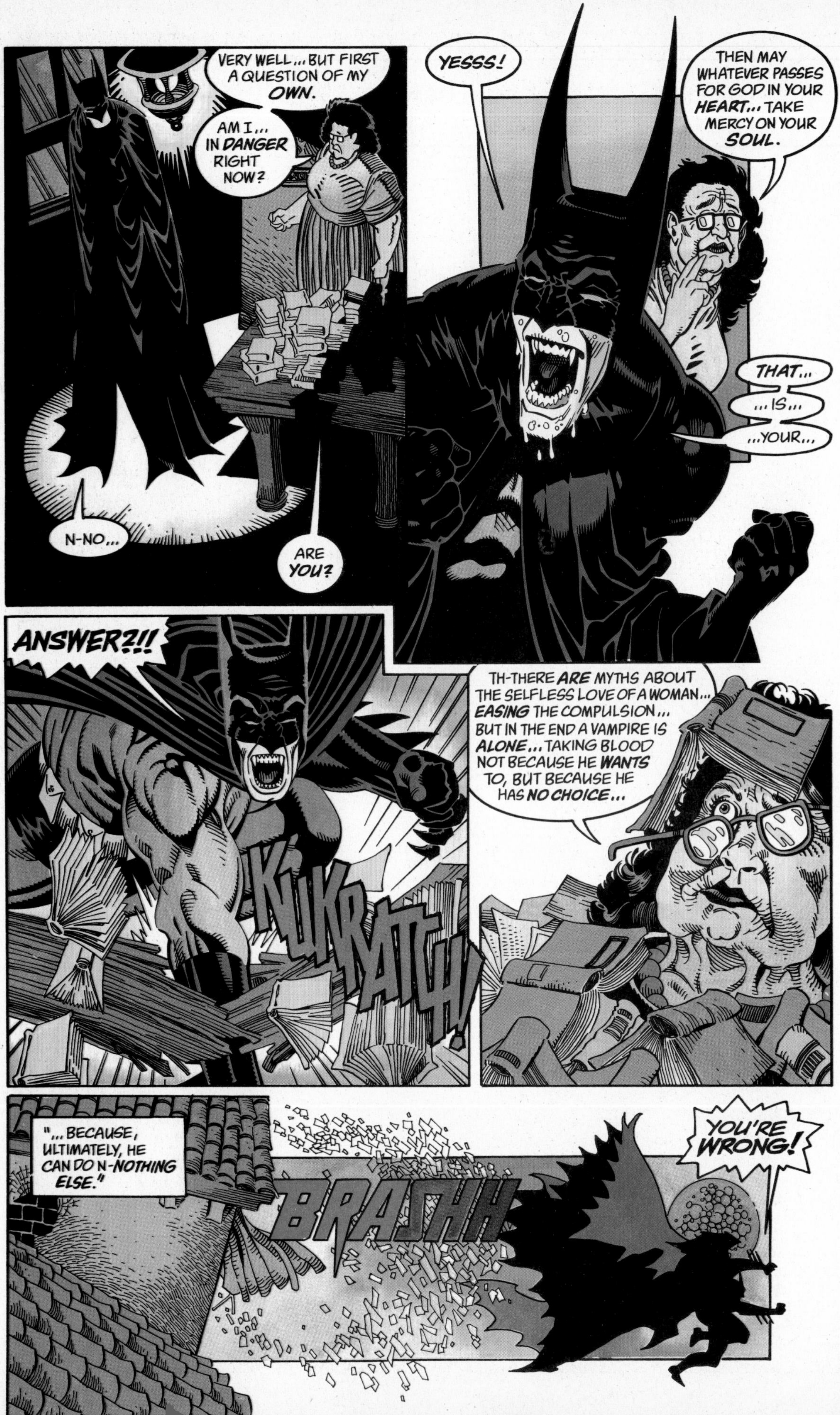
VERY WELL... BUT FIRST A QUESTION OF MY OWN.
AM I... IN DANGER RIGHT NOW?
N-NO...
ARE YOU?
YESSS!
THEN MAY WHATEVER PASSES FOR GOD IN YOUR HEART... TAKE MERCY ON YOUR SOUL.
THAT...
...IS...
...YOUR...
ANSWER?!!
KUKRATCH!
TH-THERE ARE MYTHS ABOUT THE SELFLESS LOVE OF A WOMAN... EASING THE COMPULSION... BUT IN THE END A VAMPIRE IS ALONE... TAKING BLOOD NOT BECAUSE HE WANTS TO, BUT BECAUSE HE HAS NO CHOICE...
"...BECAUSE, ULTIMATELY, HE CAN DO N-NOTHING ELSE."
BRASHH
YOU'RE WRONG!

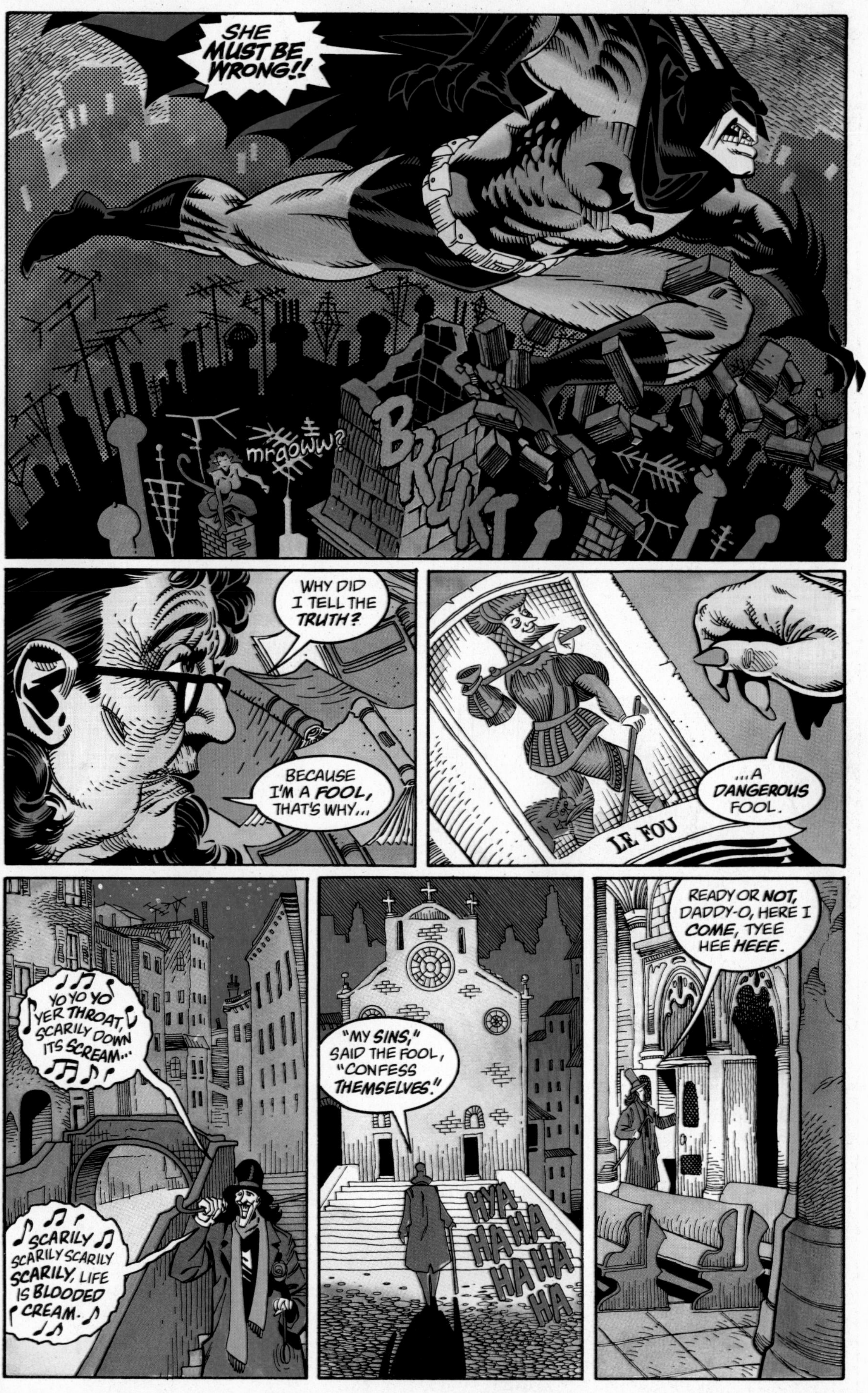
SHE MUST BE WRONG!!
BRUKT
mrgoww?
WHY DID I TELL THE TRUTH?
BECAUSE I'M A FOOL, THAT'S WHY...
LE FOU
...A DANGEROUS FOOL.
YO YO YO YER THROAT, SCARILY DOWN ITS SCREAM...
SCARILY SCARILY SCARILY SCARILY, LIFE IS BLOODED CREAM.
"MY SINS," SAID THE FOOL, "CONFESS THEMSELVES."
HYA HA HA HA HA HA HA HA
READY OR NOT, DADDY-O, HERE I COME, TYEE HEE HEEE.

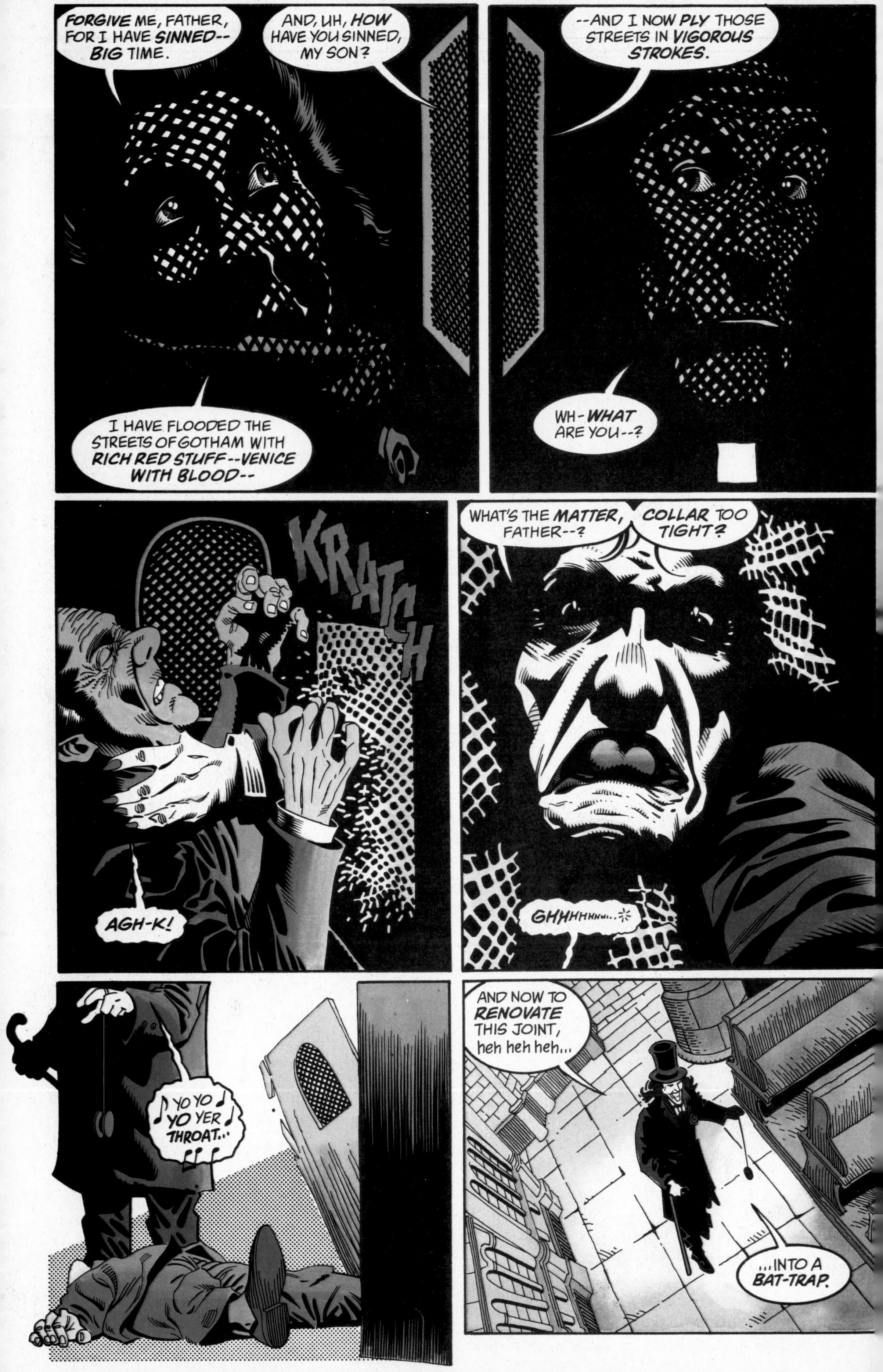
FORGIVE ME, FATHER, FOR I HAVE SINNED-- BIG TIME.
AND, UH, HOW HAVE YOU SINNED, MY SON?
I HAVE FLOODED THE STREETS OF GOTHAM WITH RICH RED STUFF--VENICE WITH BLOOD--
--AND I NOW PLY THOSE STREETS IN VIGOROUS STROKES.
WH-WHAT ARE YOU--?
KRATCH
AGH-K!
WHAT'S THE MATTER, FATHER--?
COLLAR TOO TIGHT?
GHHHHHHH...
YO YO YO YER THROAT...
AND NOW TO RENOVATE THIS JOINT, heh heh heh...
...INTO A BAT-TRAP.

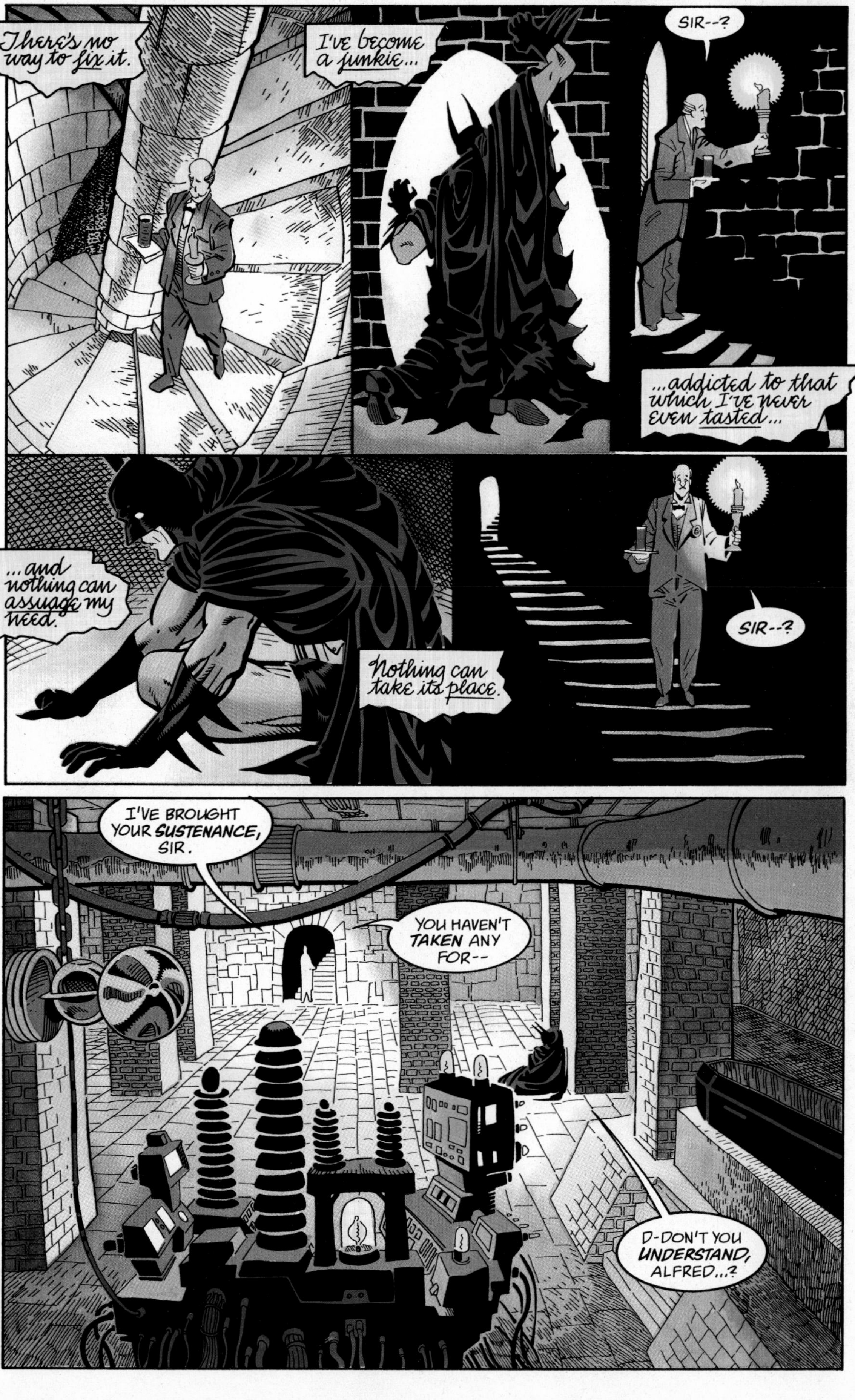
There's no way to fix it.
I've become a junkie...
SIR--?
...addicted to that which I've never even tasted...
...and nothing can assuage my need.
SIR--?
Nothing can take its place.
I'VE BROUGHT YOUR SUSTENANCE, SIR.
YOU HAVEN'T TAKEN ANY FOR--
D-DON'T YOU UNDERSTAND, ALFRED...?

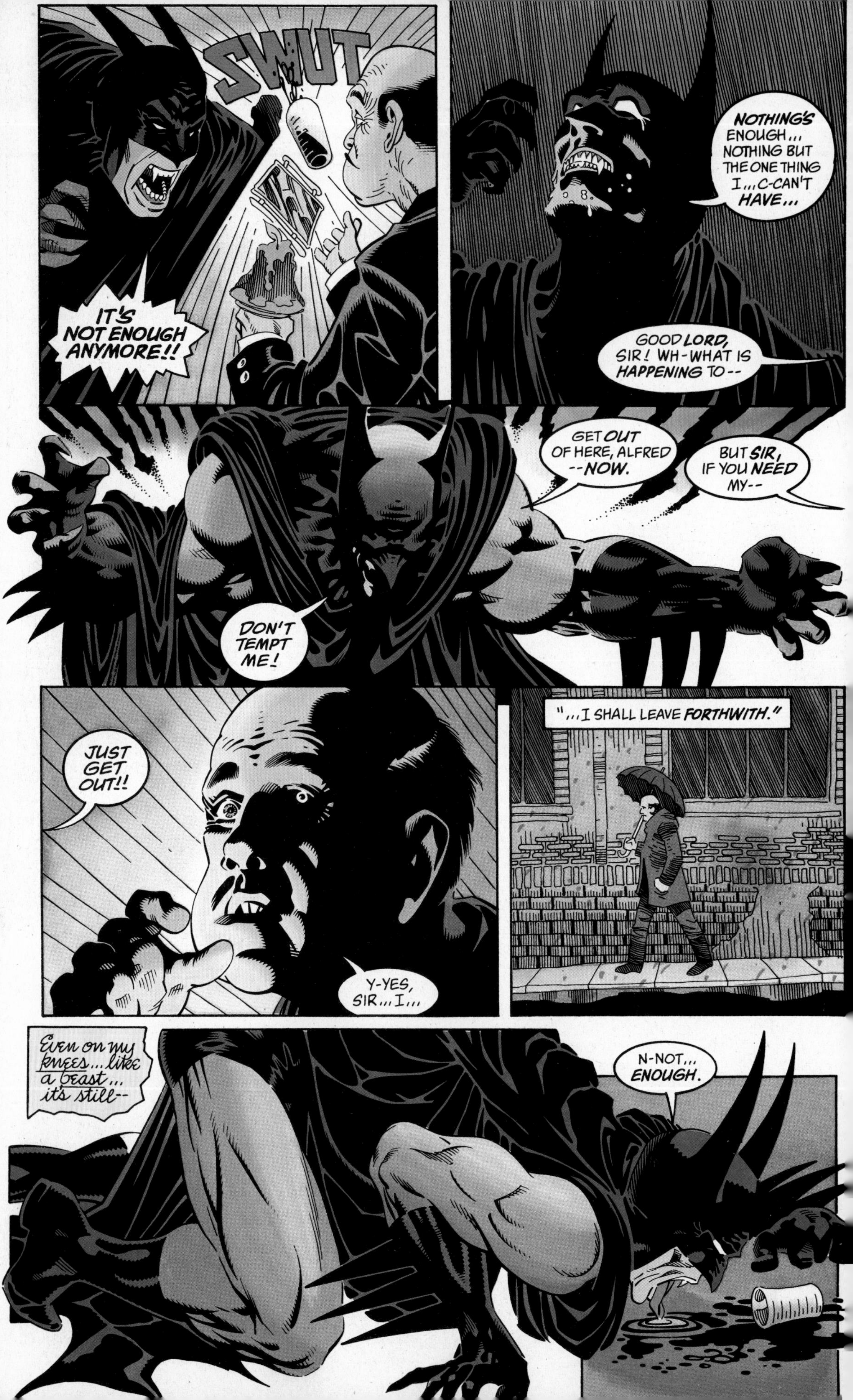
SWUT
IT'S NOT ENOUGH ANYMORE!!
NOTHING'S ENOUGH... NOTHING BUT THE ONE THING I... C-CAN'T HAVE...
GOOD LORD, SIR! WH-WHAT IS HAPPENING TO--
GET OUT OF HERE, ALFRED --NOW.
BUT SIR, IF YOU NEED MY--
DON'T TEMPT ME!
JUST GET OUT!!
Y-YES, SIR... I...
"...I SHALL LEAVE FORTHWITH."
Even on my knees... like a beast... it's still--
N-NOT... ENOUGH.

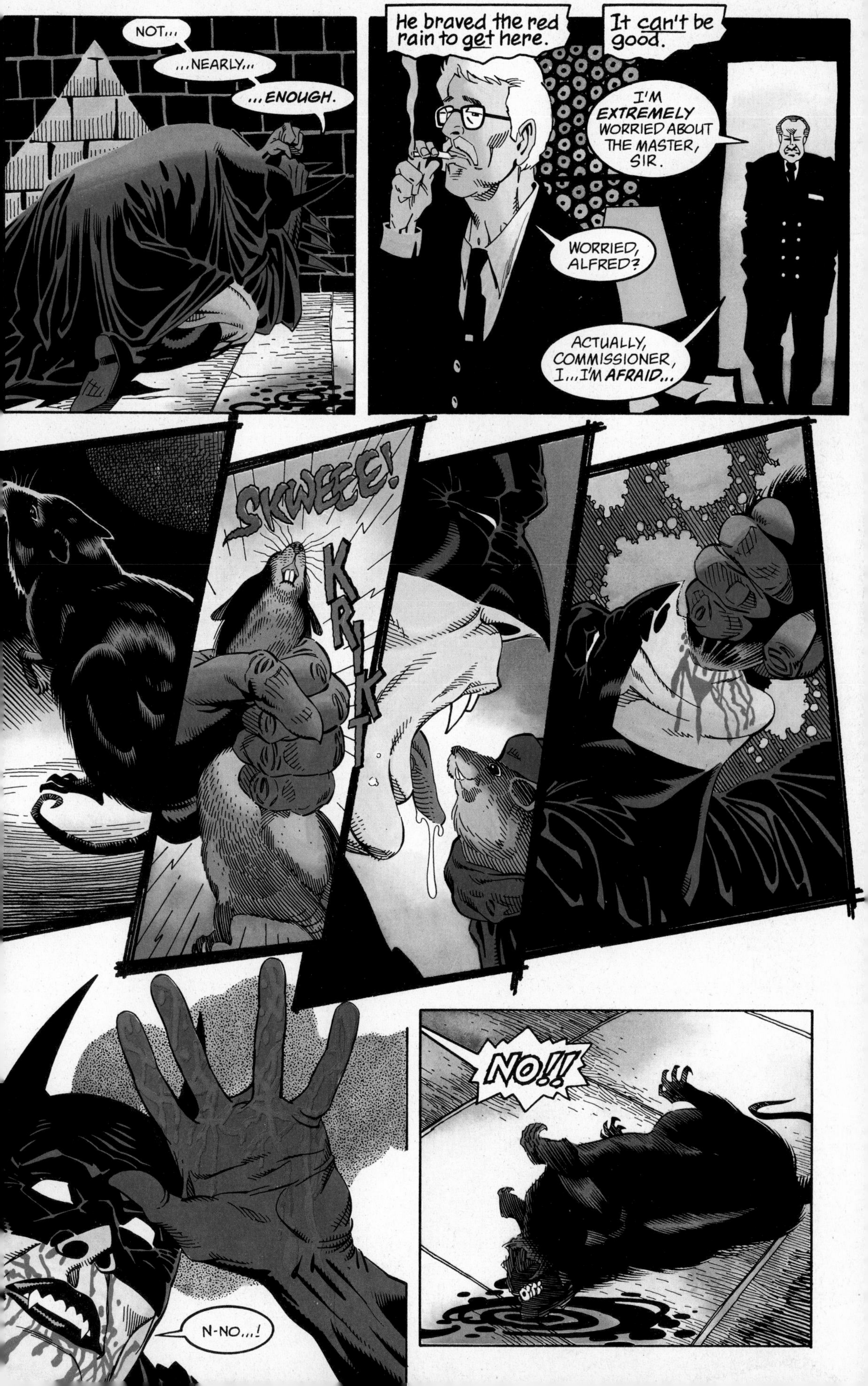
NOT...
...NEARLY...
...ENOUGH.
He braved the red rain to get here.
It can't be good.
I'M EXTREMELY WORRIED ABOUT THE MASTER, SIR.
WORRIED, ALFRED?
ACTUALLY, COMMISSIONER, I...I'M AFRAID...
SKWEEE!
KRIKT
NO!!
N-NO...!

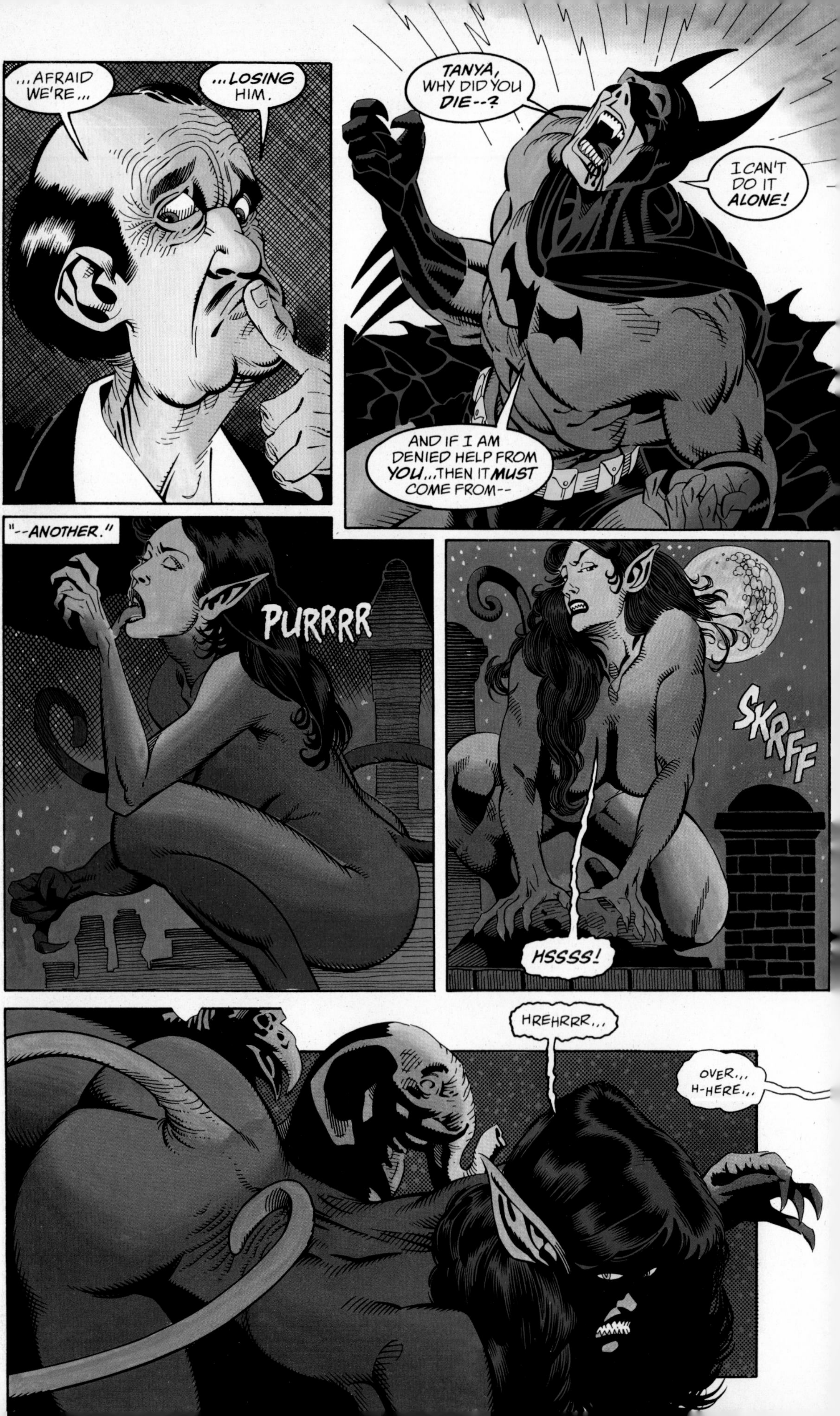
...AFRAID WE'RE...
...LOSING HIM.
TANYA, WHY DID YOU DIE--?
I CAN'T DO IT ALONE!
AND IF I AM DENIED HELP FROM YOU...THEN IT MUST COME FROM--
"--ANOTHER."
PURRRR
SKRFFF
HSSSS!
HREHRRR...
OVER... H-HERE...

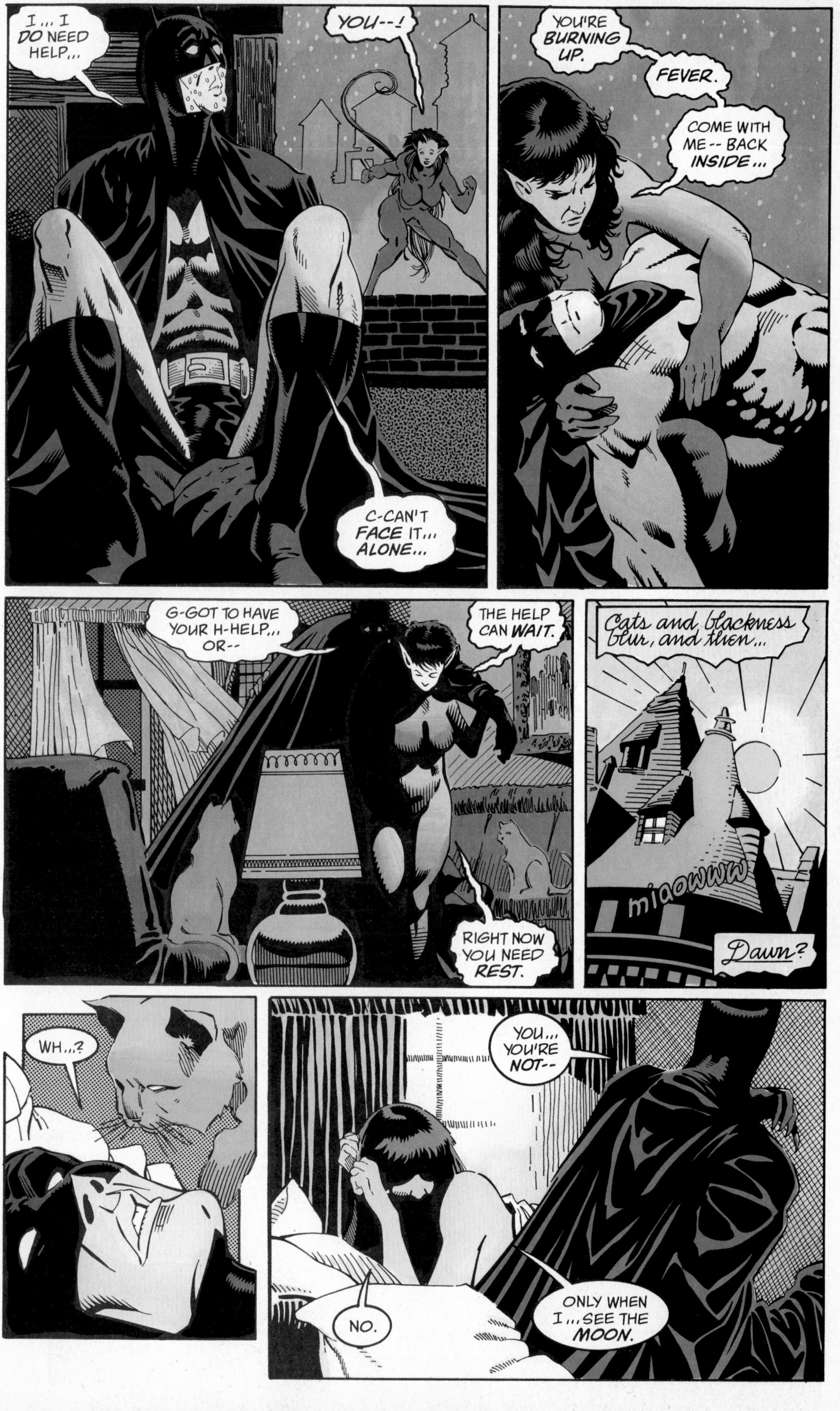
I... I DO NEED HELP...
YOU--!
C-CAN'T FACE IT... ALONE...
YOU'RE BURNING UP.
FEVER.
COME WITH ME -- BACK INSIDE...
G-GOT TO HAVE YOUR H-HELP... OR--
THE HELP CAN WAIT.
RIGHT NOW YOU NEED REST.
Cats and blackness blur, and then...
miaowww
Dawn?
WH...?
YOU... YOU'RE NOT--
NO.
ONLY WHEN I... SEE THE MOON.

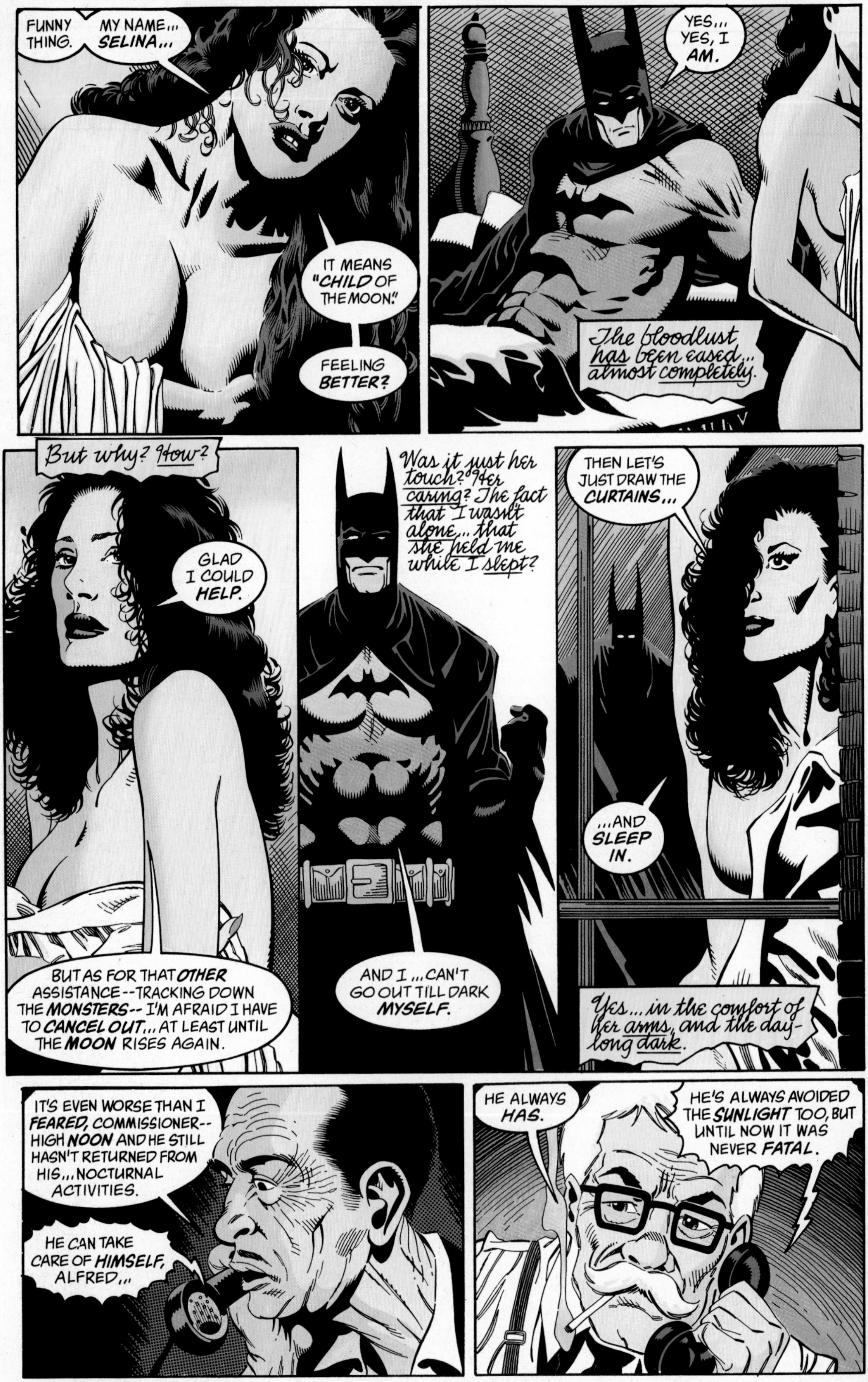
FUNNY THING.
MY NAME... SELINA...
IT MEANS "CHILD OF THE MOON."
FEELING BETTER?
YES,... YES, I AM.
The bloodlust has been eased... almost completely.
But why? How?
GLAD I COULD HELP.
BUT AS FOR THAT OTHER ASSISTANCE--TRACKING DOWN THE MONSTERS-- I'M AFRAID I HAVE TO CANCEL OUT... AT LEAST UNTIL THE MOON RISES AGAIN.
Was it just her touch? Her caring? The fact that I wasn't alone... that she held me while I slept?
AND I ... CAN'T GO OUT TILL DARK MYSELF.
THEN LET'S JUST DRAW THE CURTAINS...
...AND SLEEP IN.
Yes... in the comfort of her arms, and the day-long dark.
IT'S EVEN WORSE THAN I FEARED, COMMISSIONER-- HIGH NOON AND HE STILL HASN'T RETURNED FROM HIS... NOCTURNAL ACTIVITIES.
HE CAN TAKE CARE OF HIMSELF, ALFRED...
HE ALWAYS HAS.
HE'S ALWAYS AVOIDED THE SUNLIGHT TOO, BUT UNTIL NOW IT WAS NEVER FATAL.

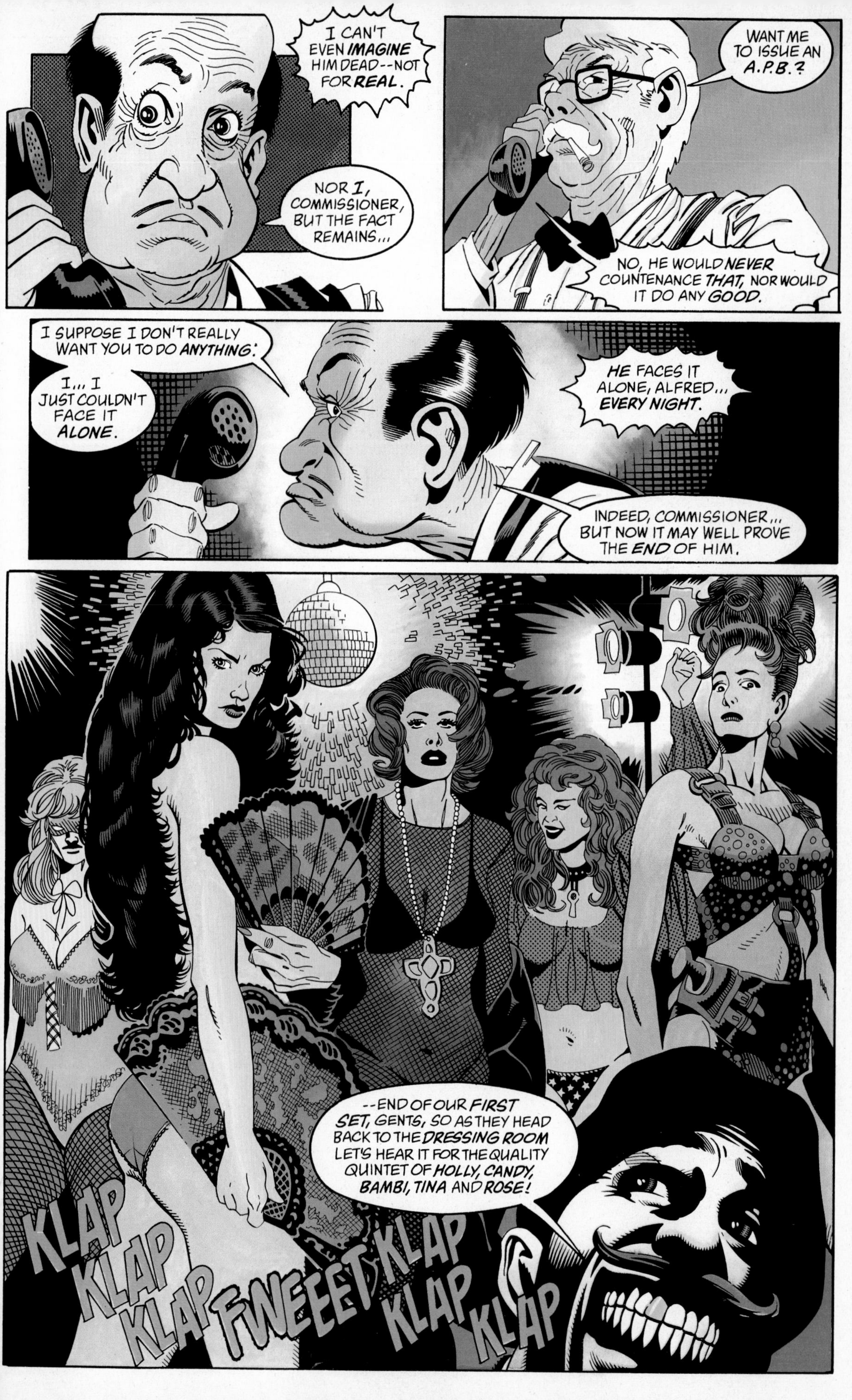
I CAN'T EVEN IMAGINE HIM DEAD--NOT FOR REAL.
NOR I, COMMISSIONER, BUT THE FACT REMAINS...
WANT ME TO ISSUE AN A.P.B.?
NO, HE WOULD NEVER COUNTENANCE THAT, NOR WOULD IT DO ANY GOOD.
I SUPPOSE I DON'T REALLY WANT YOU TO DO ANYTHING.
I... I JUST COULDN'T FACE IT ALONE.
HE FACES IT ALONE, ALFRED... EVERY NIGHT.
INDEED, COMMISSIONER... BUT NOW IT MAY WELL PROVE THE END OF HIM.
--END OF OUR FIRST SET, GENTS, SO AS THEY HEAD BACK TO THE DRESSING ROOM LET'S HEAR IT FOR THE QUALITY QUINTET OF HOLLY, CANDY, BAMBI, TINA AND ROSE!
KLAP KLAP KLAP
FWEEET
KLAP KLAP KLAP

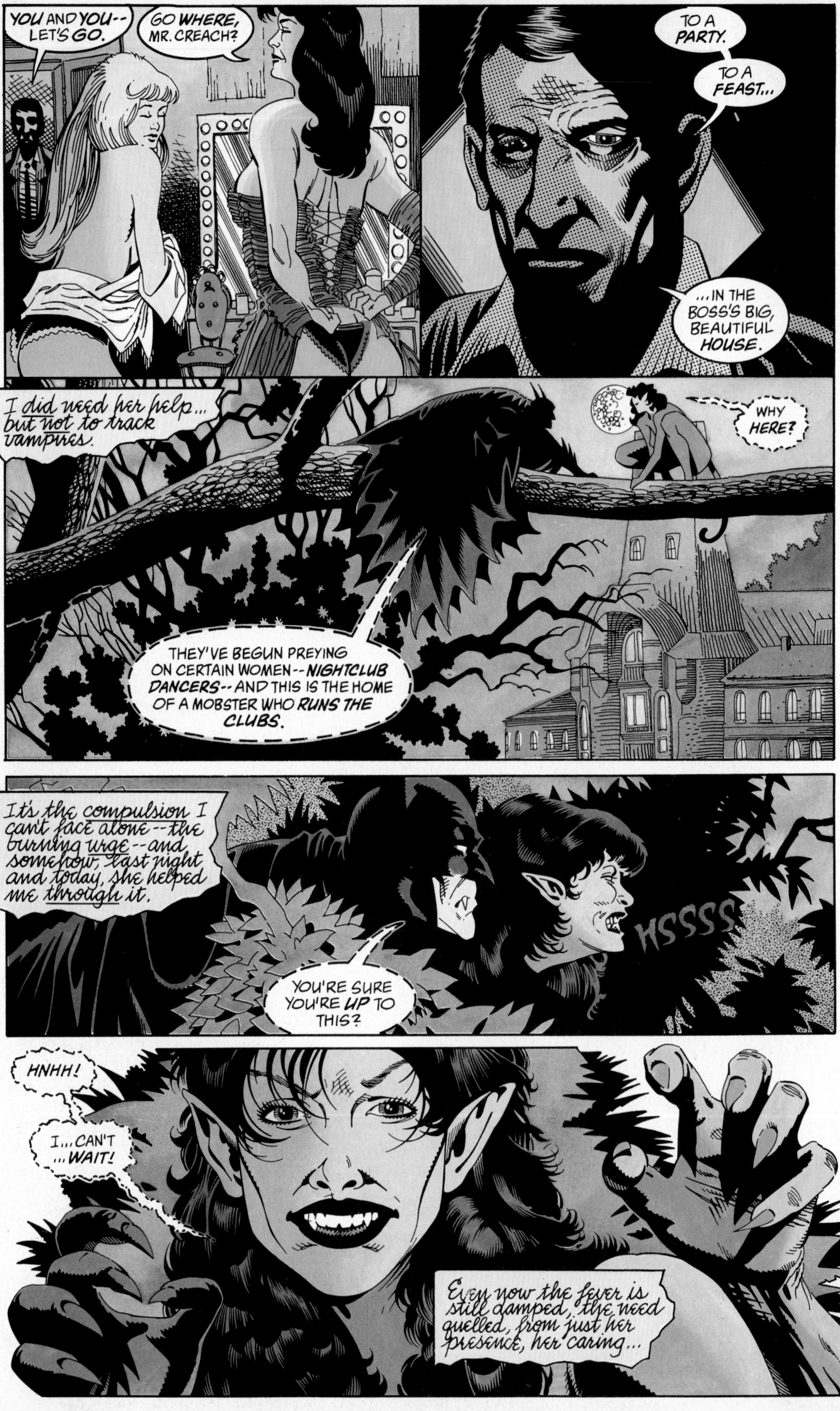
YOU AND YOU--
LET'S GO.
GO WHERE,
MR. CREACH?
TO A
PARTY.
TO A
FEAST...
...IN THE
BOSS'S BIG,
BEAUTIFUL
HOUSE.
I did need her help...
but not to track
vampires.
WHY
HERE?
THEY'VE BEGUN PREYING
ON CERTAIN WOMEN--NIGHTCLUB
DANCERS--AND THIS IS THE HOME
OF A MOBSTER WHO RUNS THE
CLUBS.
It's the compulsion I
can't face alone--the
burning urge--and
somehow, last night
and today, she helped
me through it.
HSSSSH
YOU'RE SURE
YOU'RE UP TO
THIS?
HNHH!
I...CAN'T
...WAIT!
Even now the fever is
still damped, the need
quelled, from just her
presence, her caring...

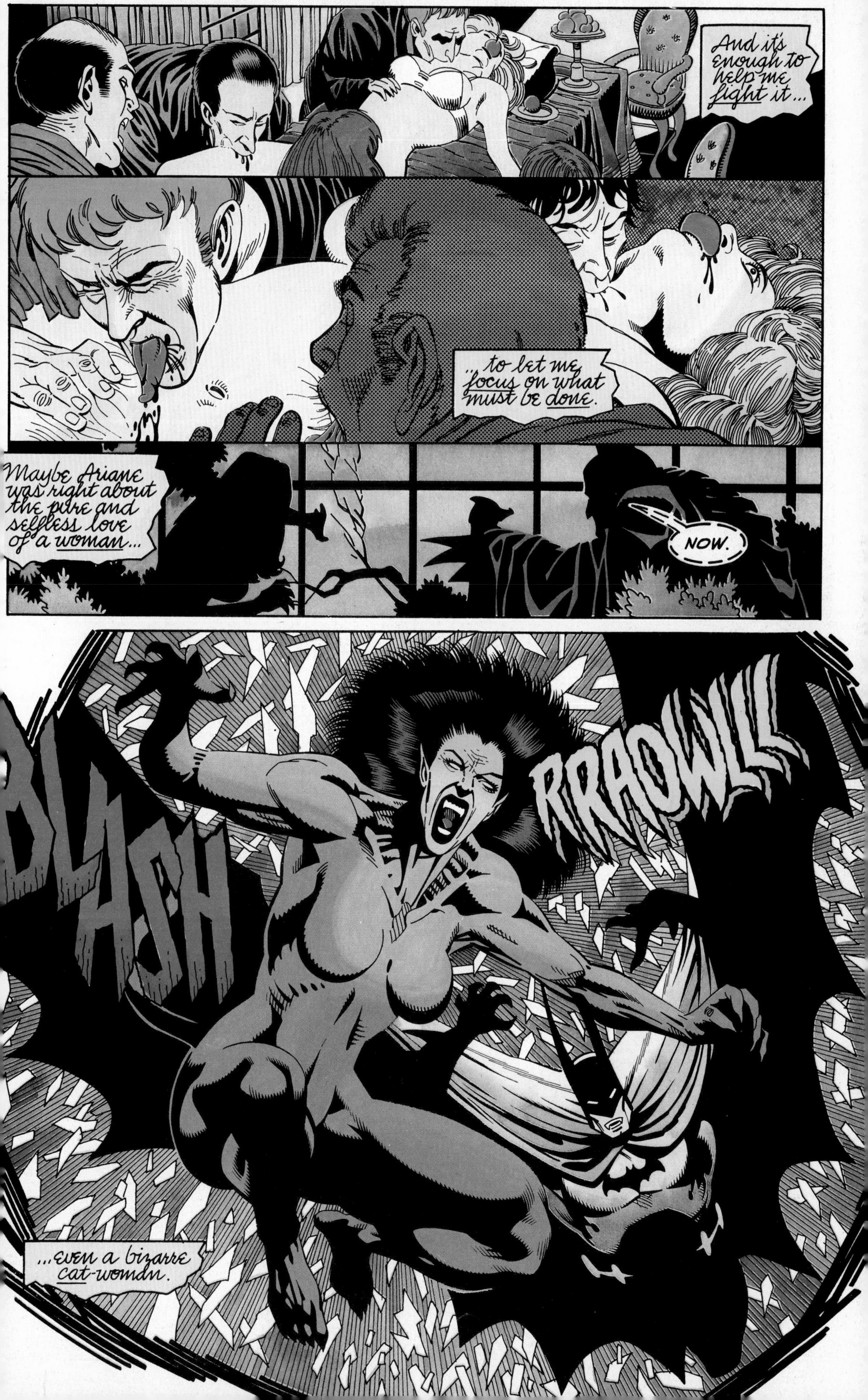
And it's enough to help me fight it...
...to let me focus on what must be done.
Maybe Ariane was right about the pure and selfless love of a woman...
NOW.
BLASH
RRAOWLL
...even a bizarre cat-woman.

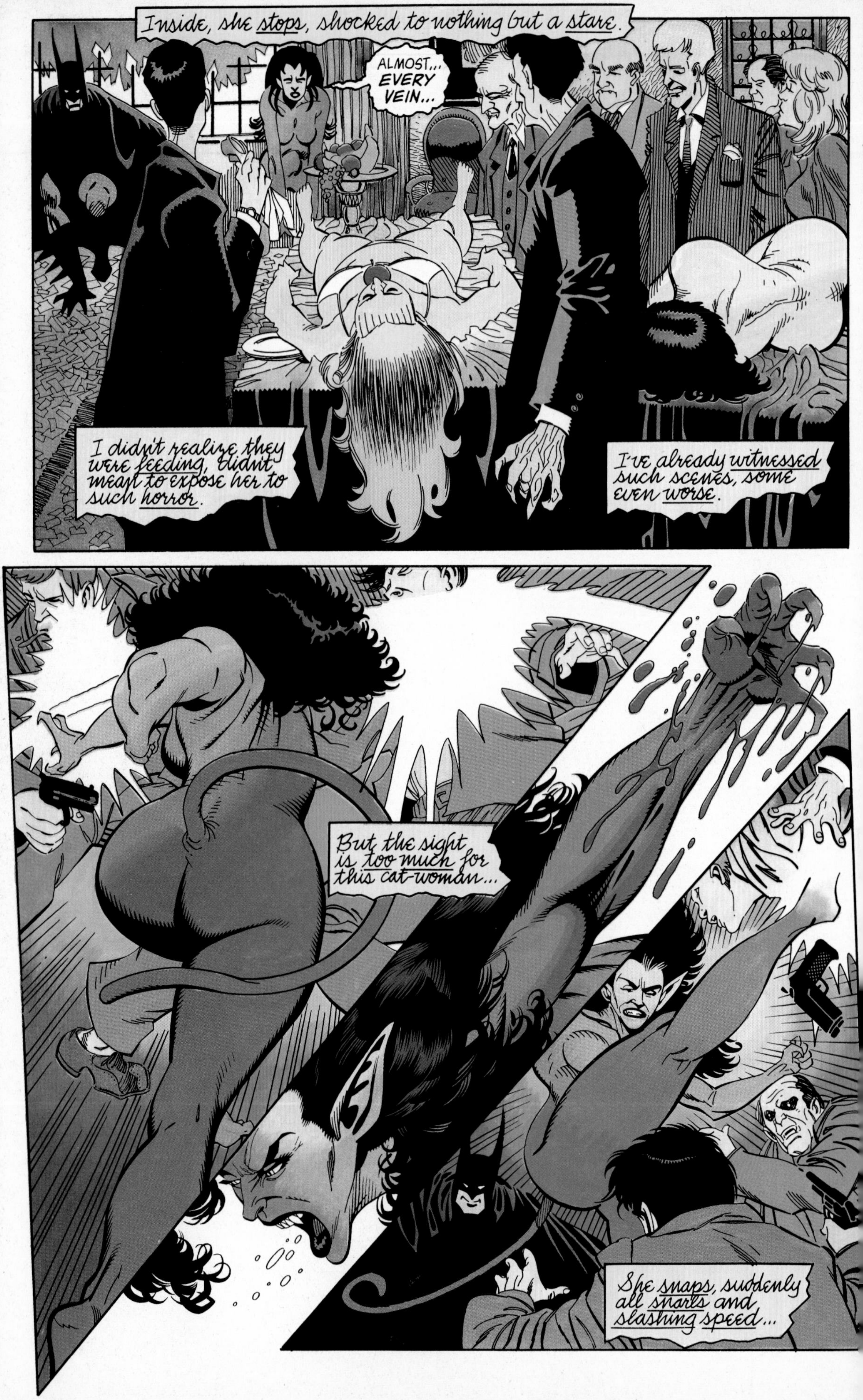
Inside, she stops, shocked to nothing but a stare.
ALMOST... EVERY VEIN...
I didn't realize they were feeding, didn't mean to expose her to such horror.
I've already witnessed such scenes, some even worse.
But the sight is too much for this cat-woman...
She snaps, suddenly all snarls and slashing speed...

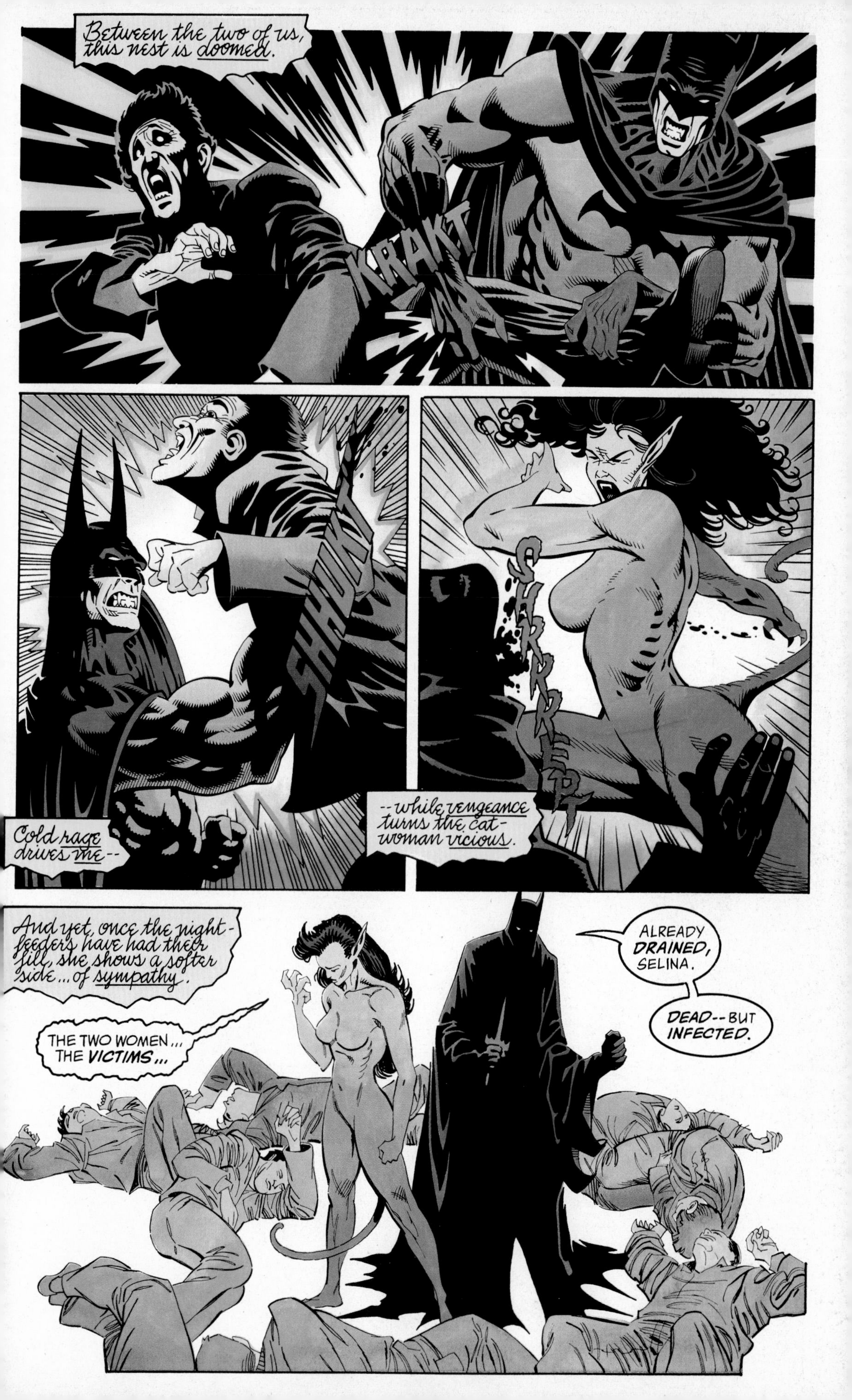

Between the two of us, this nest is doomed.
KRAKT
SHHUKT
Cold rage drives the--
--while vengeance turns the cat-woman vicious.
SHRRRRPT
And yet, once the night-feeders have had their fill, she shows a softer side... of sympathy.
THE TWO WOMEN... THE VICTIMS...
ALREADY DRAINED, SELINA.
DEAD--BUT INFECTED.

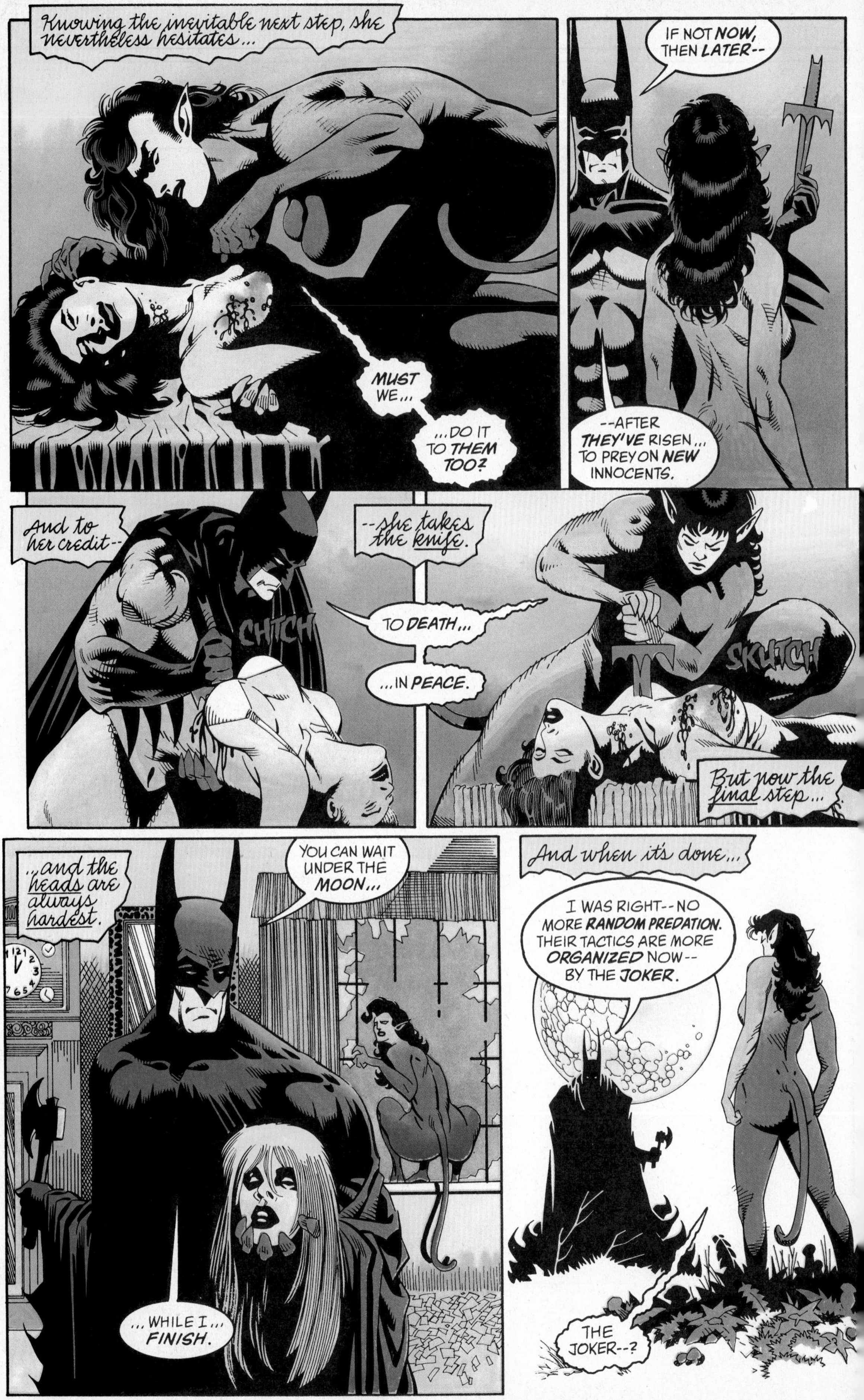
Knowing the inevitable next step, she nevertheless hesitates...
MUST WE...
...DO IT TO THEM TOO?
IF NOT NOW, THEN LATER--
--AFTER THEY'VE RISEN... TO PREY ON NEW INNOCENTS.
And to her credit--
CHTCH
--she takes the knife.
TO DEATH...
...IN PEACE.
SKUTCH
But now the final step...
...and the heads are always hardest.
YOU CAN WAIT UNDER THE MOON...
...WHILE I... FINISH.
And when it's done...
I WAS RIGHT--NO MORE RANDOM PREDATION. THEIR TACTICS ARE MORE ORGANIZED NOW-- BY THE JOKER.
THE JOKER--?

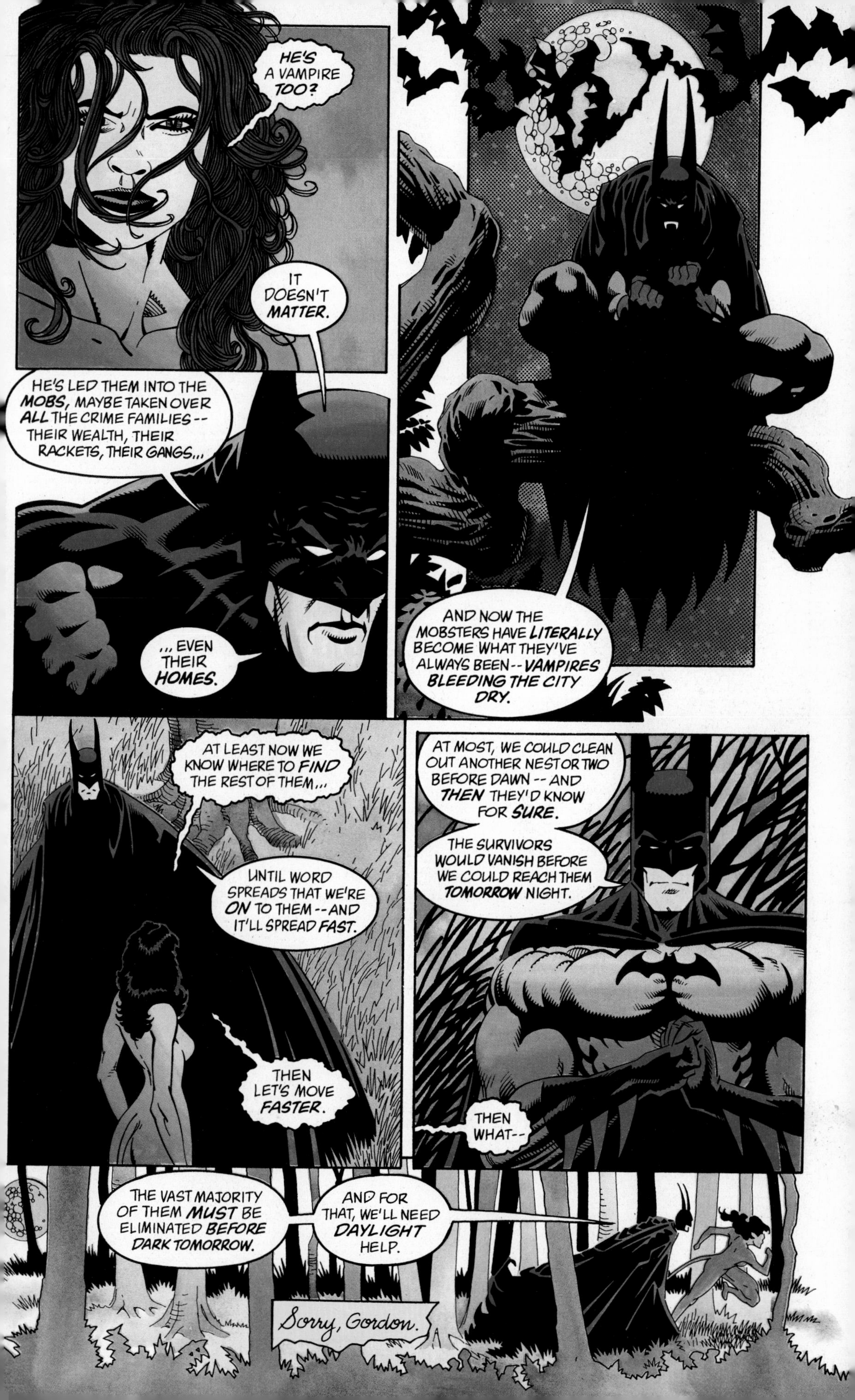
HE'S A VAMPIRE TOO?
IT DOESN'T MATTER.
HE'S LED THEM INTO THE MOBS, MAYBE TAKEN OVER ALL THE CRIME FAMILIES -- THEIR WEALTH, THEIR RACKETS, THEIR GANGS...
... EVEN THEIR HOMES.
AND NOW THE MOBSTERS HAVE LITERALLY BECOME WHAT THEY'VE ALWAYS BEEN -- VAMPIRES BLEEDING THE CITY DRY.
AT LEAST NOW WE KNOW WHERE TO FIND THE REST OF THEM...
UNTIL WORD SPREADS THAT WE'RE ON TO THEM -- AND IT'LL SPREAD FAST.
THEN LET'S MOVE FASTER.
AT MOST, WE COULD CLEAN OUT ANOTHER NEST OR TWO BEFORE DAWN -- AND THEN THEY'D KNOW FOR SURE.
THE SURVIVORS WOULD VANISH BEFORE WE COULD REACH THEM TOMORROW NIGHT.
THEN WHAT--
THE VAST MAJORITY OF THEM MUST BE ELIMINATED BEFORE DARK TOMORROW.
AND FOR THAT, WE'LL NEED DAYLIGHT HELP.
Sorry, Gordon.

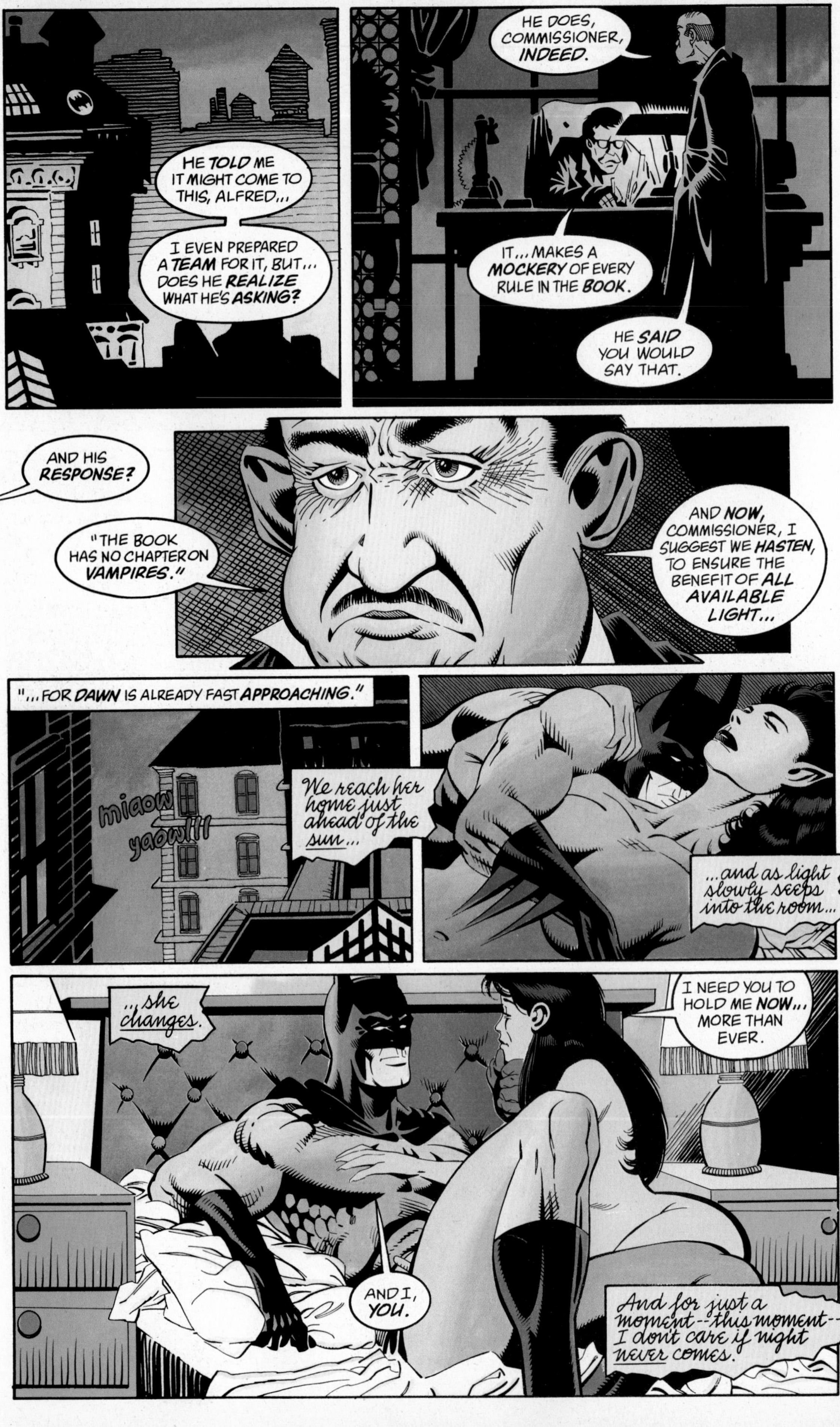
HE TOLD ME IT MIGHT COME TO THIS, ALFRED...
I EVEN PREPARED A TEAM FOR IT, BUT... DOES HE REALIZE WHAT HE'S ASKING?
HE DOES, COMMISSIONER, INDEED.
IT... MAKES A MOCKERY OF EVERY RULE IN THE BOOK.
HE SAID YOU WOULD SAY THAT.
AND HIS RESPONSE?
"THE BOOK HAS NO CHAPTER ON VAMPIRES."
AND NOW, COMMISSIONER, I SUGGEST WE HASTEN, TO ENSURE THE BENEFIT OF ALL AVAILABLE LIGHT...
"...FOR DAWN IS ALREADY FAST APPROACHING."
miaow
yaowl!!
We reach her home just ahead of the sun...
...and as light slowly seeps into the room...
...she changes.
I NEED YOU TO HOLD ME NOW... MORE THAN EVER.
AND I, YOU.
And for just a moment--this moment--I don't care if night never comes.

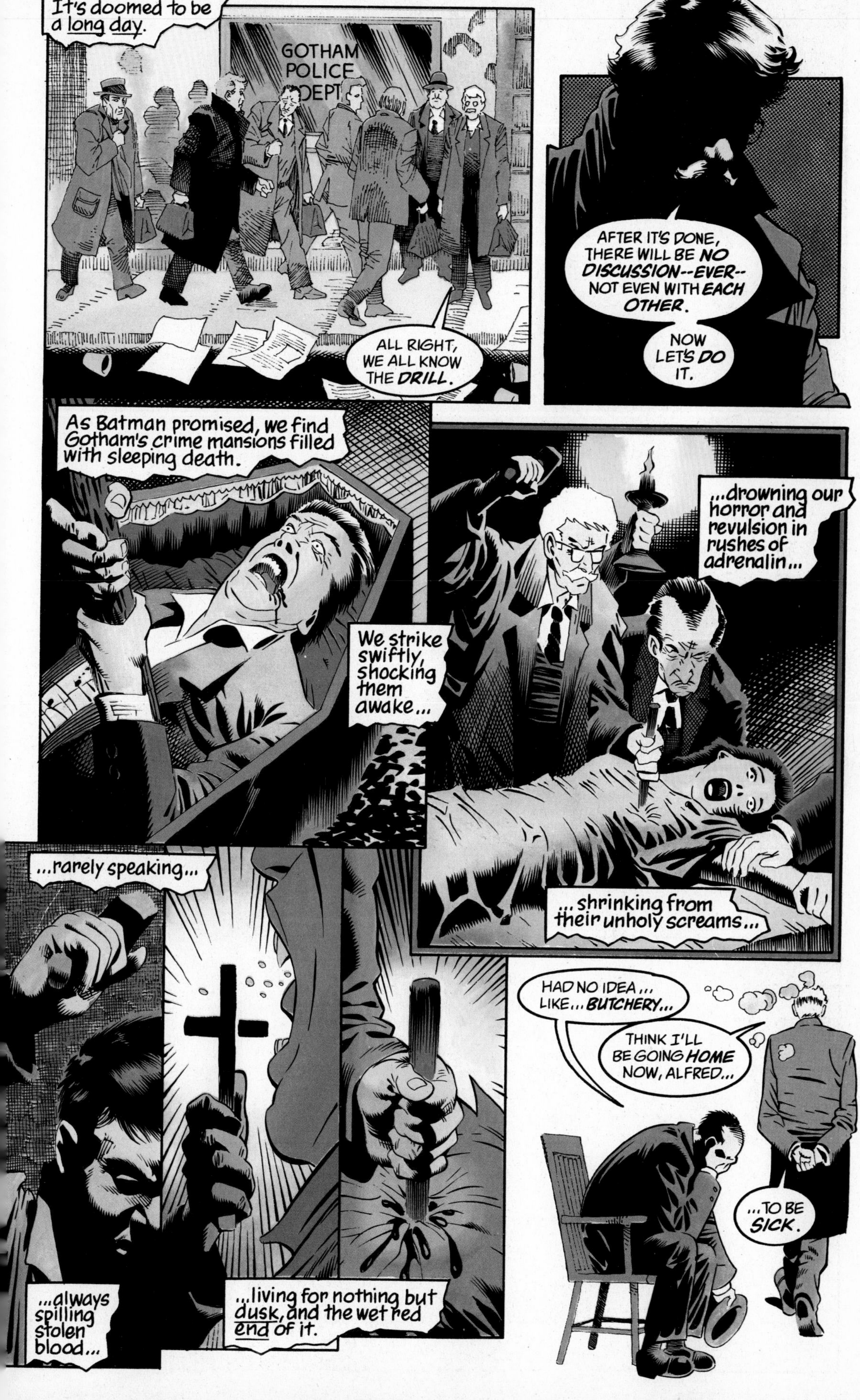
It's doomed to be a long day.
GOTHAM POLICE DEPT
ALL RIGHT, WE ALL KNOW THE DRILL.
AFTER IT'S DONE, THERE WILL BE NO DISCUSSION--EVER-- NOT EVEN WITH EACH OTHER.
NOW LET'S DO IT.
As Batman promised, we find Gotham's crime mansions filled with sleeping death.
We strike swiftly, shocking them awake...
...drowning our horror and revulsion in rushes of adrenalin...
...shrinking from their unholy screams...
...rarely speaking...
...always spilling stolen blood...
...living for nothing but dusk, and the wet red end of it.
HAD NO IDEA... LIKE... BUTCHERY...
THINK I'LL BE GOING HOME NOW, ALFRED...
...TO BE SICK.

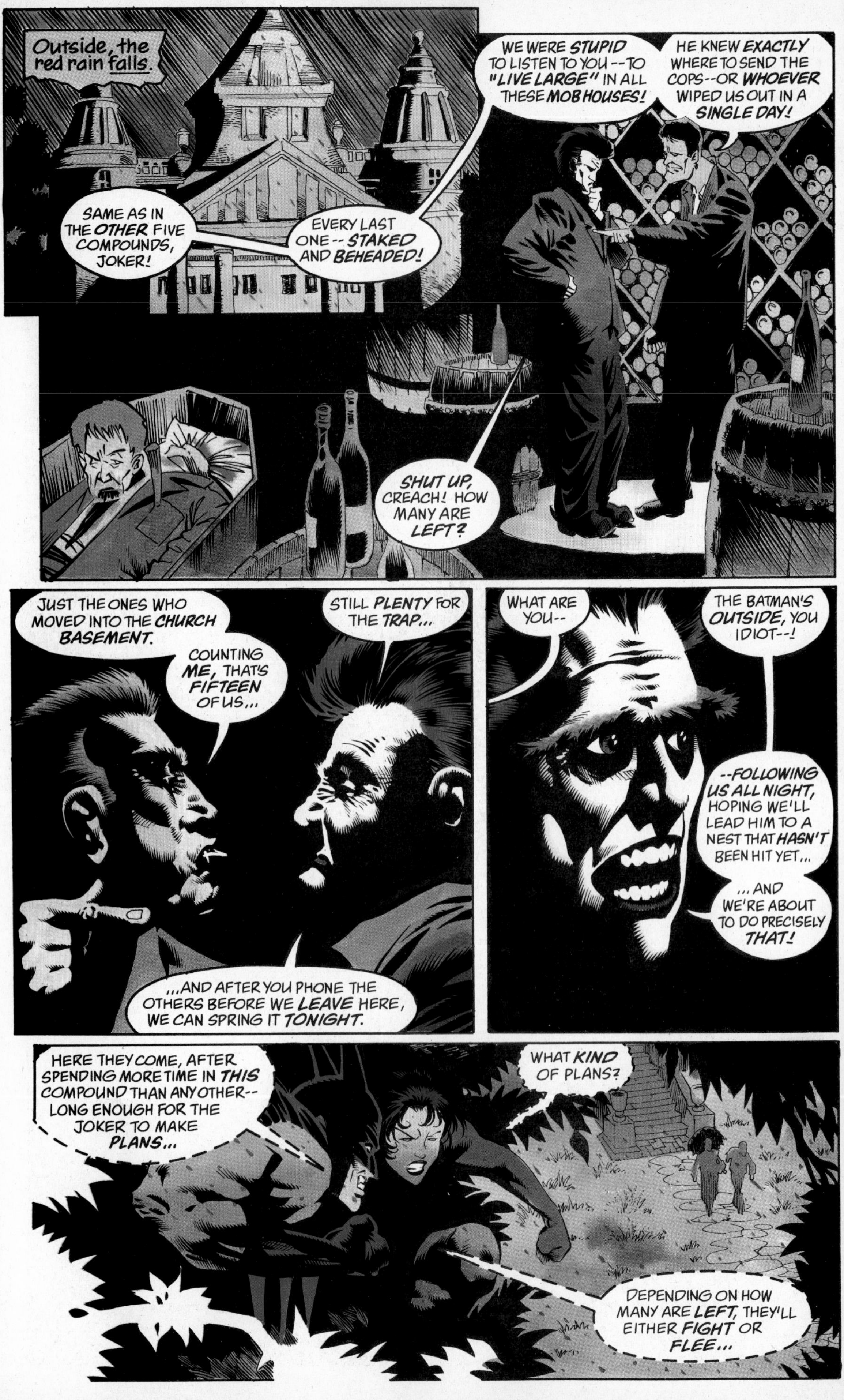
Outside, the red rain falls.
SAME AS IN THE OTHER FIVE COMPOUNDS, JOKER!
EVERY LAST ONE-- STAKED AND BEHEADED!
WE WERE STUPID TO LISTEN TO YOU --TO "LIVE LARGE" IN ALL THESE MOB HOUSES!
HE KNEW EXACTLY WHERE TO SEND THE COPS--OR WHOEVER WIPED US OUT IN A SINGLE DAY!
SHUT UP, CREACH! HOW MANY ARE LEFT?
JUST THE ONES WHO MOVED INTO THE CHURCH BASEMENT.
COUNTING ME, THAT'S FIFTEEN OF US...
STILL PLENTY FOR THE TRAP...
...AND AFTER YOU PHONE THE OTHERS BEFORE WE LEAVE HERE, WE CAN SPRING IT TONIGHT.
WHAT ARE YOU--
THE BATMAN'S OUTSIDE, YOU IDIOT--!
--FOLLOWING US ALL NIGHT, HOPING WE'LL LEAD HIM TO A NEST THAT HASN'T BEEN HIT YET...
...AND WE'RE ABOUT TO DO PRECISELY THAT!
HERE THEY COME, AFTER SPENDING MORE TIME IN THIS COMPOUND THAN ANY OTHER-- LONG ENOUGH FOR THE JOKER TO MAKE PLANS...
WHAT KIND OF PLANS?
DEPENDING ON HOW MANY ARE LEFT, THEY'LL EITHER FIGHT OR FLEE...

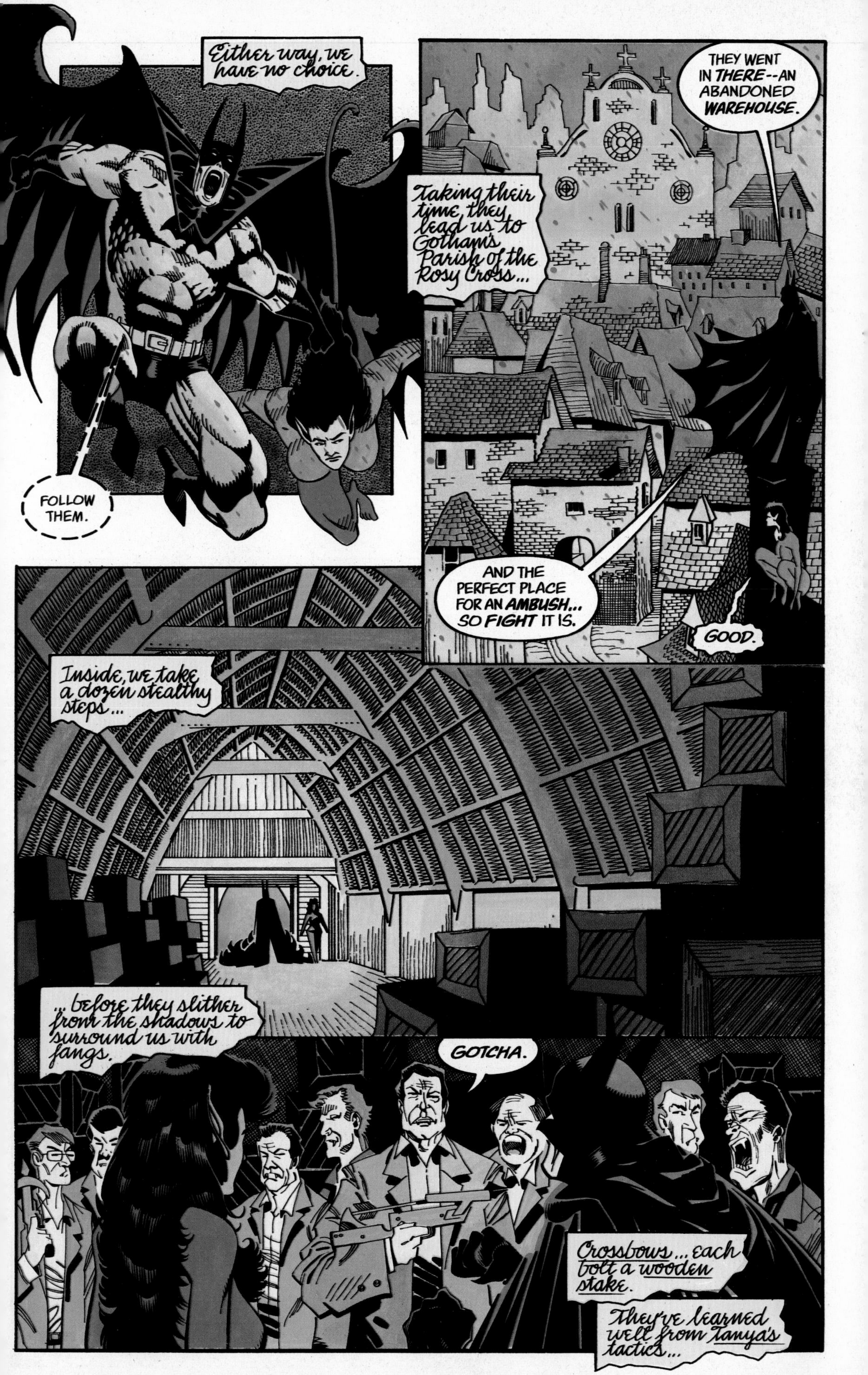

Either way, we have no choice.
FOLLOW THEM.
THEY WENT IN THERE--AN ABANDONED WAREHOUSE.
Taking their time, they lead us to Gotham's Parish of the Rosy Cross...
AND THE PERFECT PLACE FOR AN AMBUSH... SO FIGHT IT IS.
GOOD.
Inside, we take a dozen stealthy steps...
...before they slither from the shadows to surround us with fangs.
GOTCHA.
Crossbows... each bolt a wooden stake.
They've learned well from Tanya's tactics...

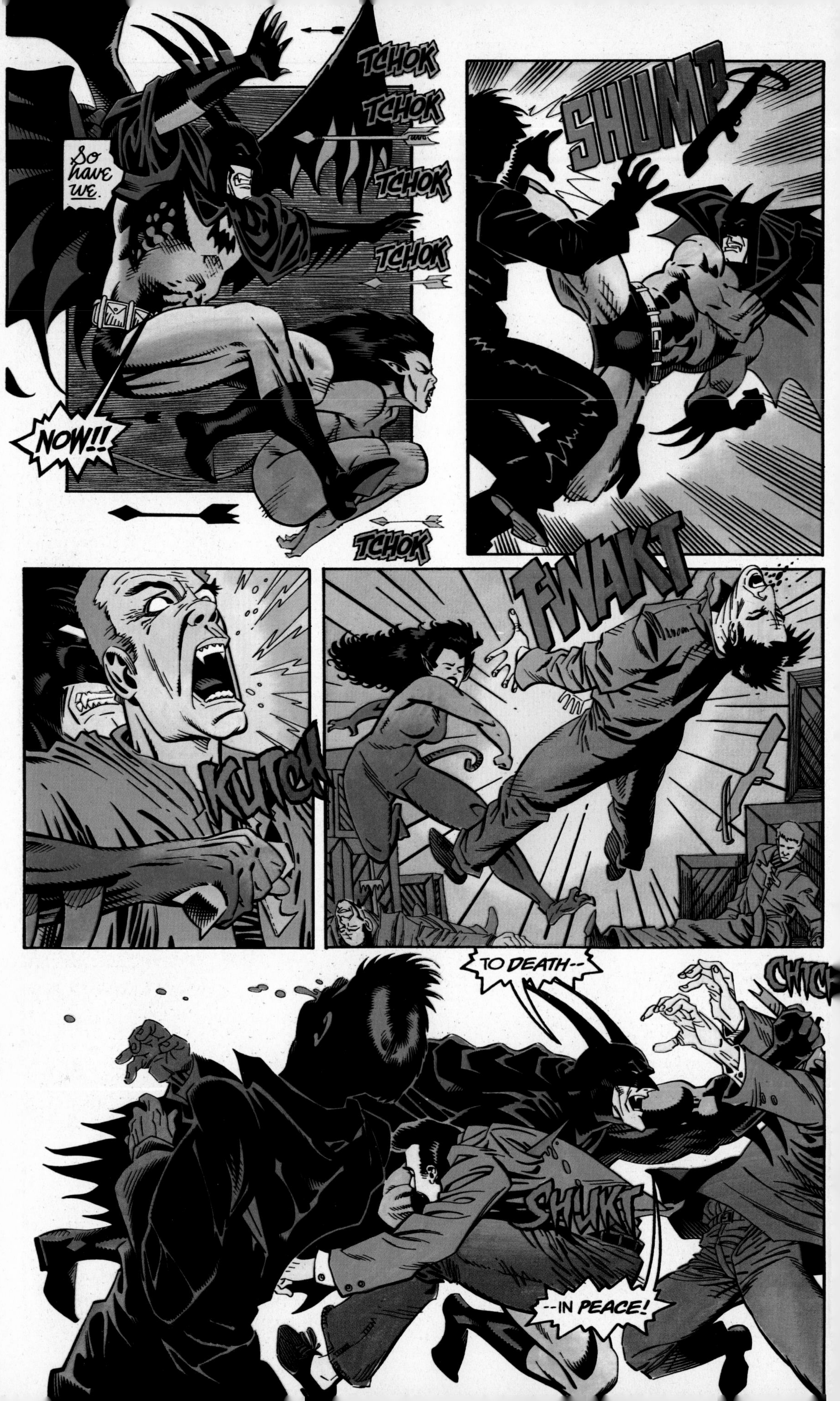

TCHOK
TCHOK
So have we.
TCHOK
TCHOK
NOW!!
TCHOK
SHUMP
KUTCH
FWAKT
TO DEATH--
CHTCH
SHUKT
--IN PEACE!

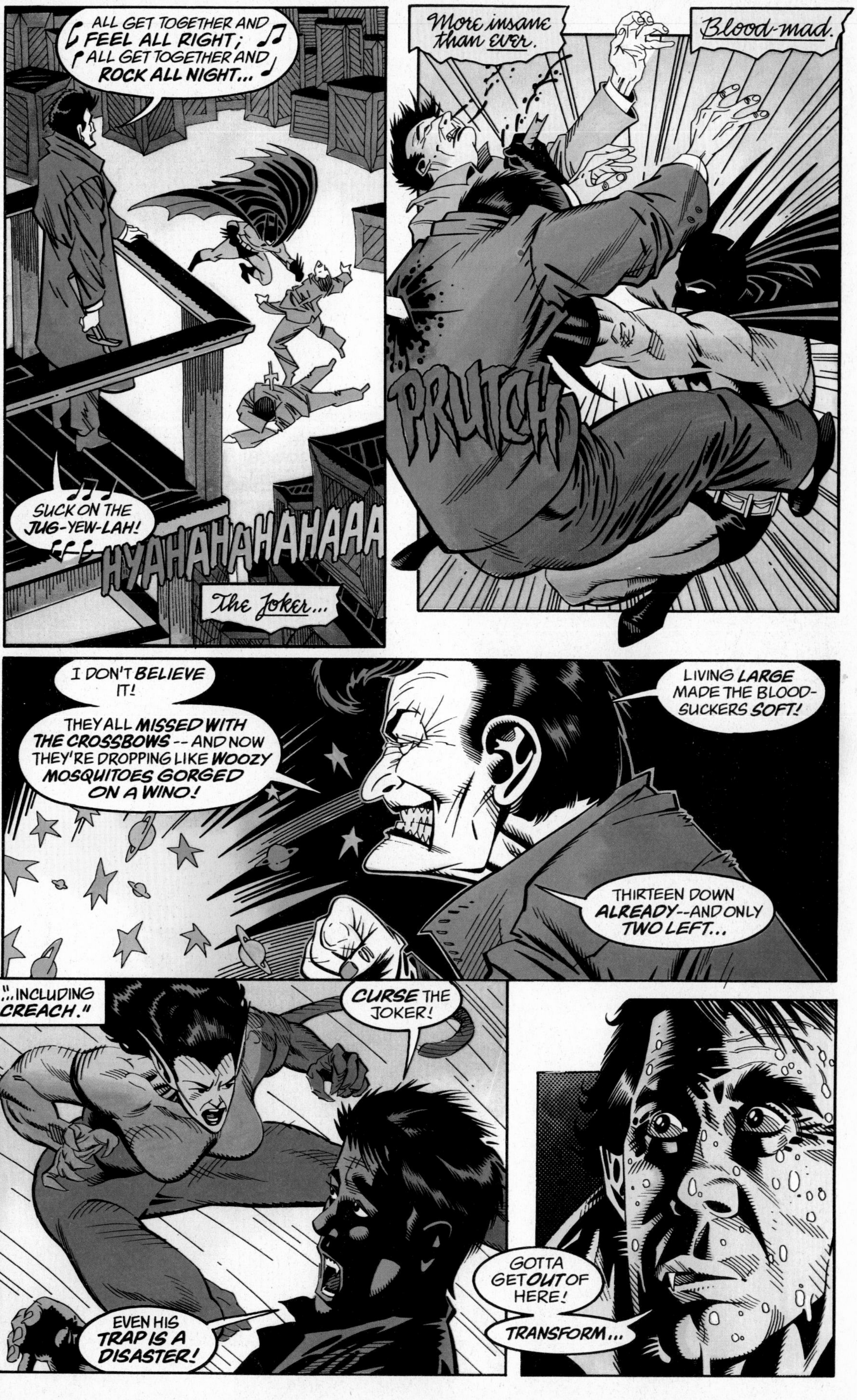
ALL GET TOGETHER AND FEEL ALL RIGHT; ALL GET TOGETHER AND ROCK ALL NIGHT...
SUCK ON THE JUG-YEW-LAH!
HYAHAHAHAHAAA
The Joker...
More insane than ever.
Blood-mad.
PRUTCH
I DON'T BELIEVE IT!
THEY ALL MISSED WITH THE CROSSBOWS -- AND NOW THEY'RE DROPPING LIKE WOOZY MOSQUITOES GORGED ON A WINO!
LIVING LARGE MADE THE BLOOD-SUCKERS SOFT!
THIRTEEN DOWN ALREADY--AND ONLY TWO LEFT...
"...INCLUDING CREACH."
CURSE THE JOKER!
EVEN HIS TRAP IS A DISASTER!
GOTTA GET OUT OF HERE!
TRANSFORM...

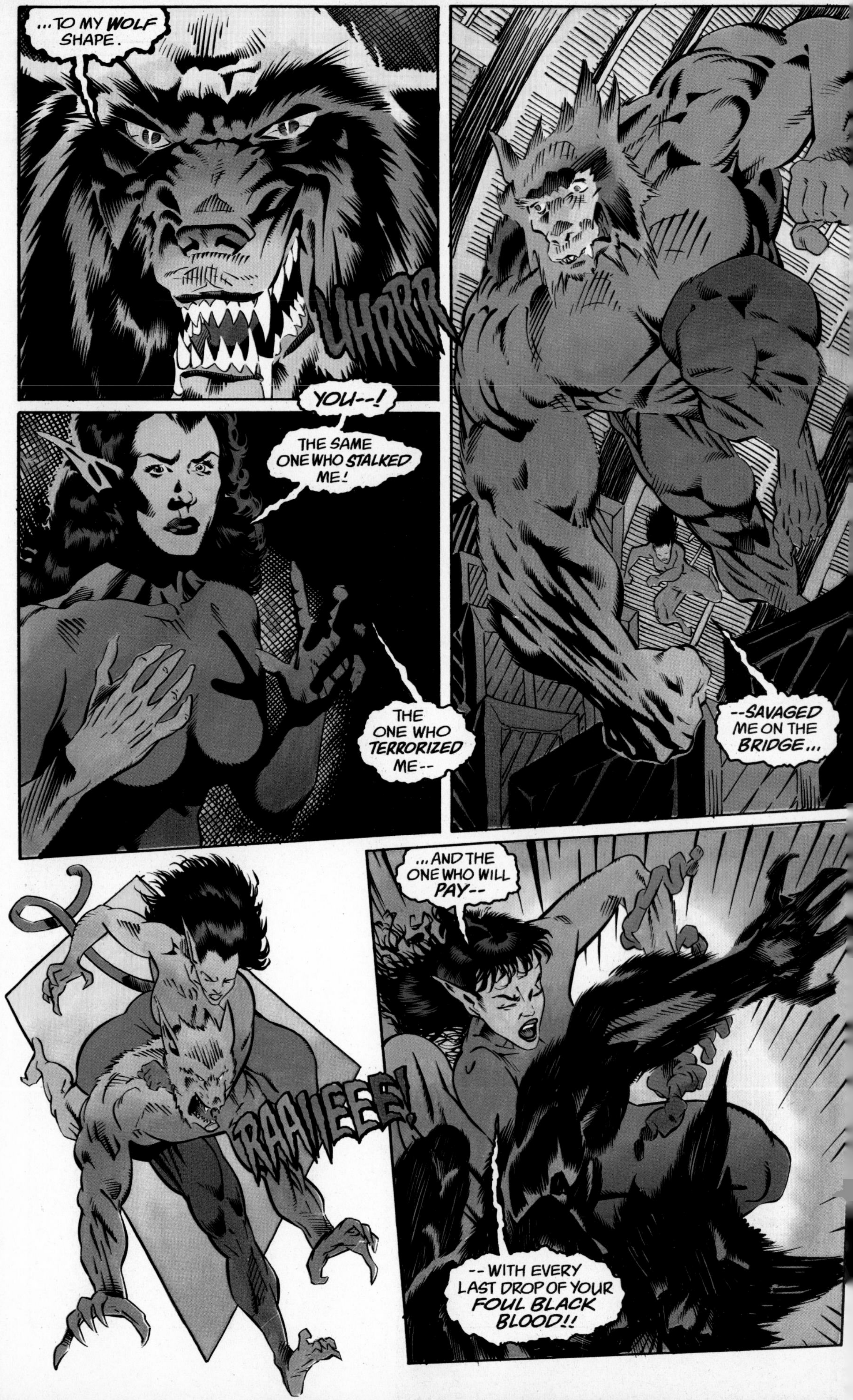
...TO MY WOLF SHAPE.
UHRRR
YOU--!
THE SAME ONE WHO STALKED ME!
THE ONE WHO TERRORIZED ME--
--SAVAGED ME ON THE BRIDGE...
...AND THE ONE WHO WILL PAY--
RAAIEEE!
--WITH EVERY LAST DROP OF YOUR FOUL BLACK BLOOD!!

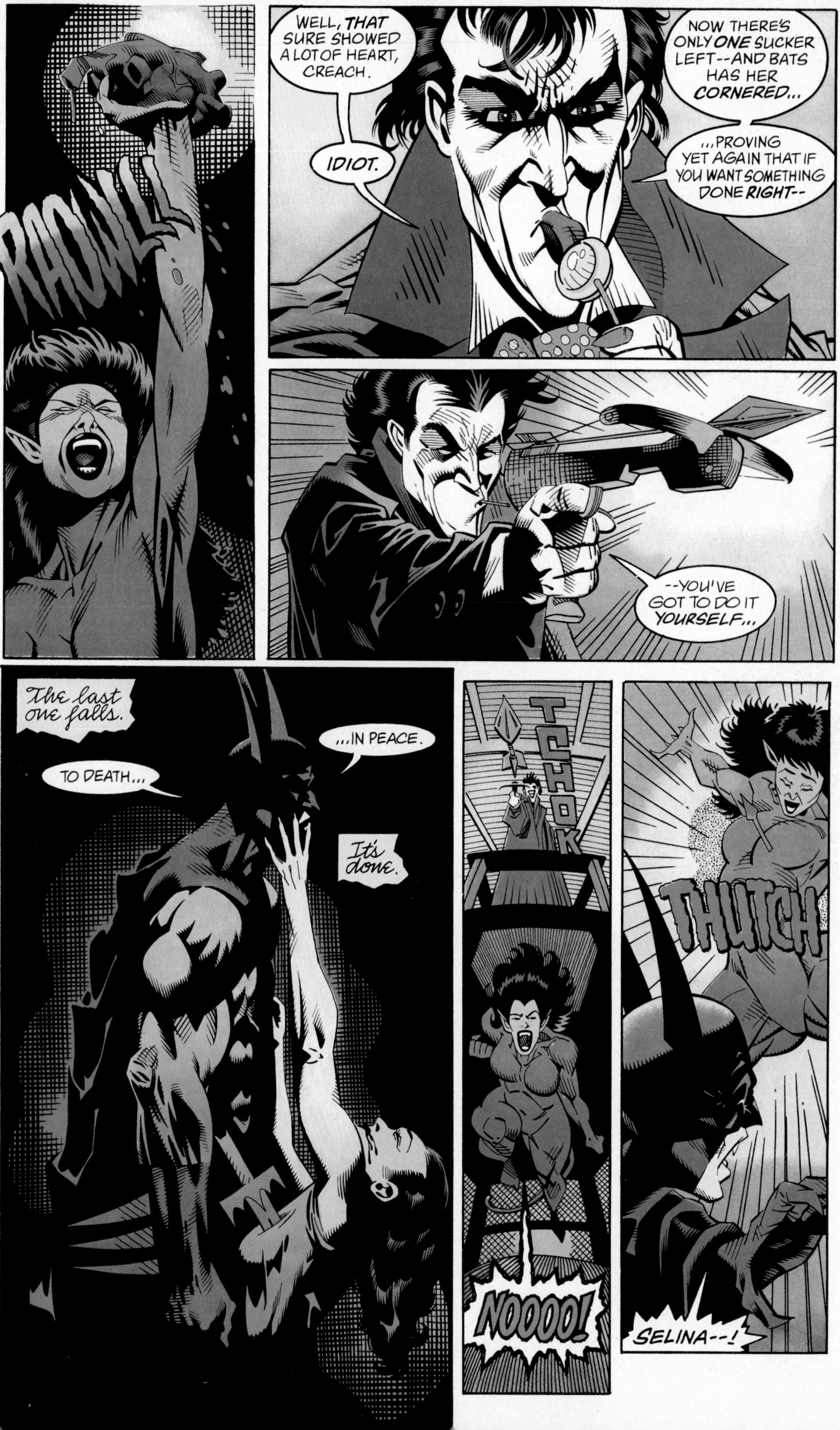
RAOWL!
WELL, THAT SURE SHOWED A LOT OF HEART, CREACH.
IDIOT.
NOW THERE'S ONLY ONE SUCKER LEFT--AND BATS HAS HER CORNERED...
...PROVING YET AGAIN THAT IF YOU WANT SOMETHING DONE RIGHT--
--YOU'VE GOT TO DO IT YOURSELF...
TCHOK
NOOOO!
THUTCH
SELINA--!
The last one falls.
TO DEATH...
...IN PEACE.
It's done.

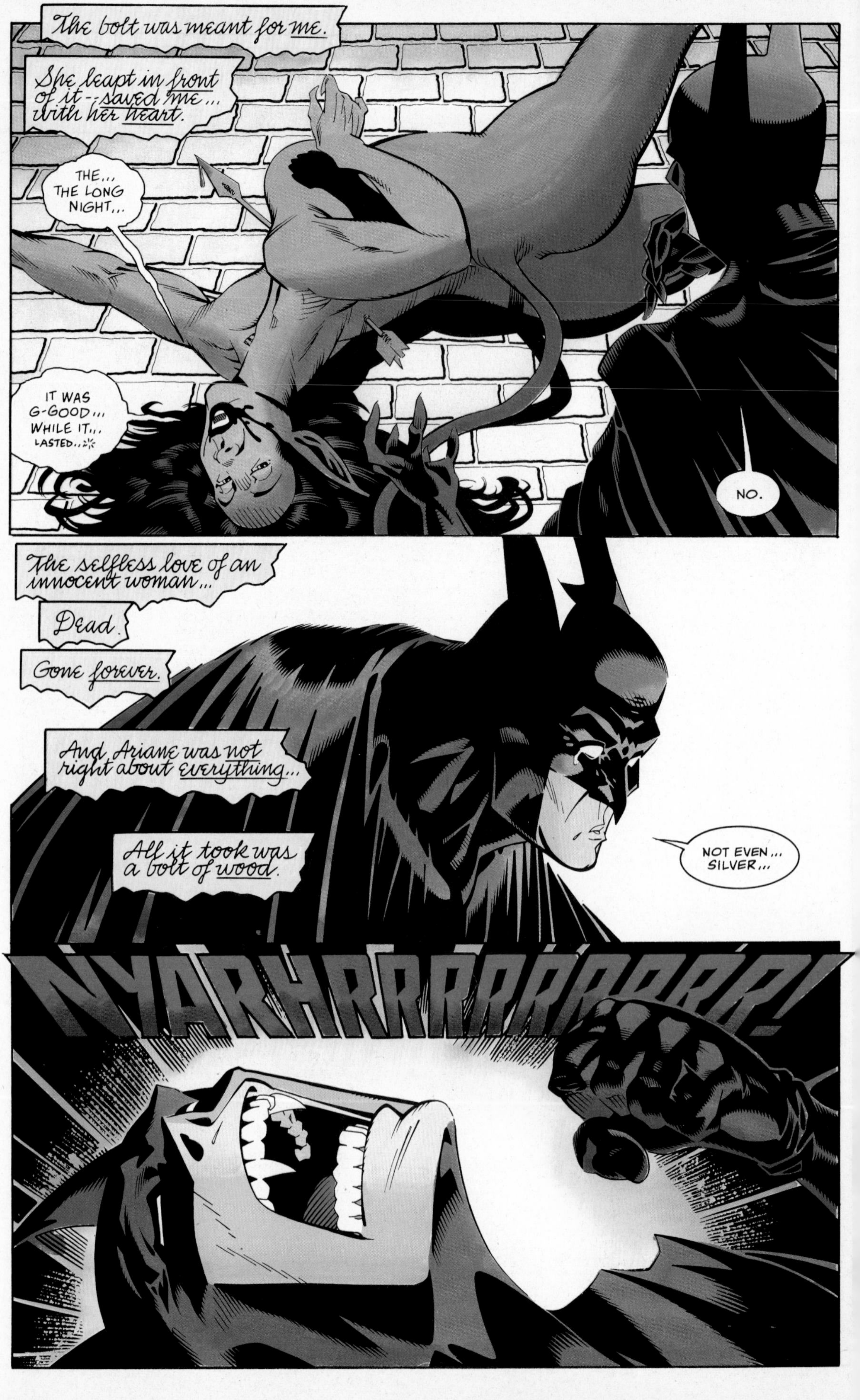
The bolt was meant for me.
She leapt in front of it--saved me... with her heart.
THE... THE LONG NIGHT...
IT WAS G-GOOD... WHILE IT... LASTED...
NO.
The selfless love of an innocent woman...
Dead.
Gone forever.
And Ariane was not right about everything...
All it took was a bolt of wood.
NOT EVEN... SILVER...
NYARHRRRRRRRR!

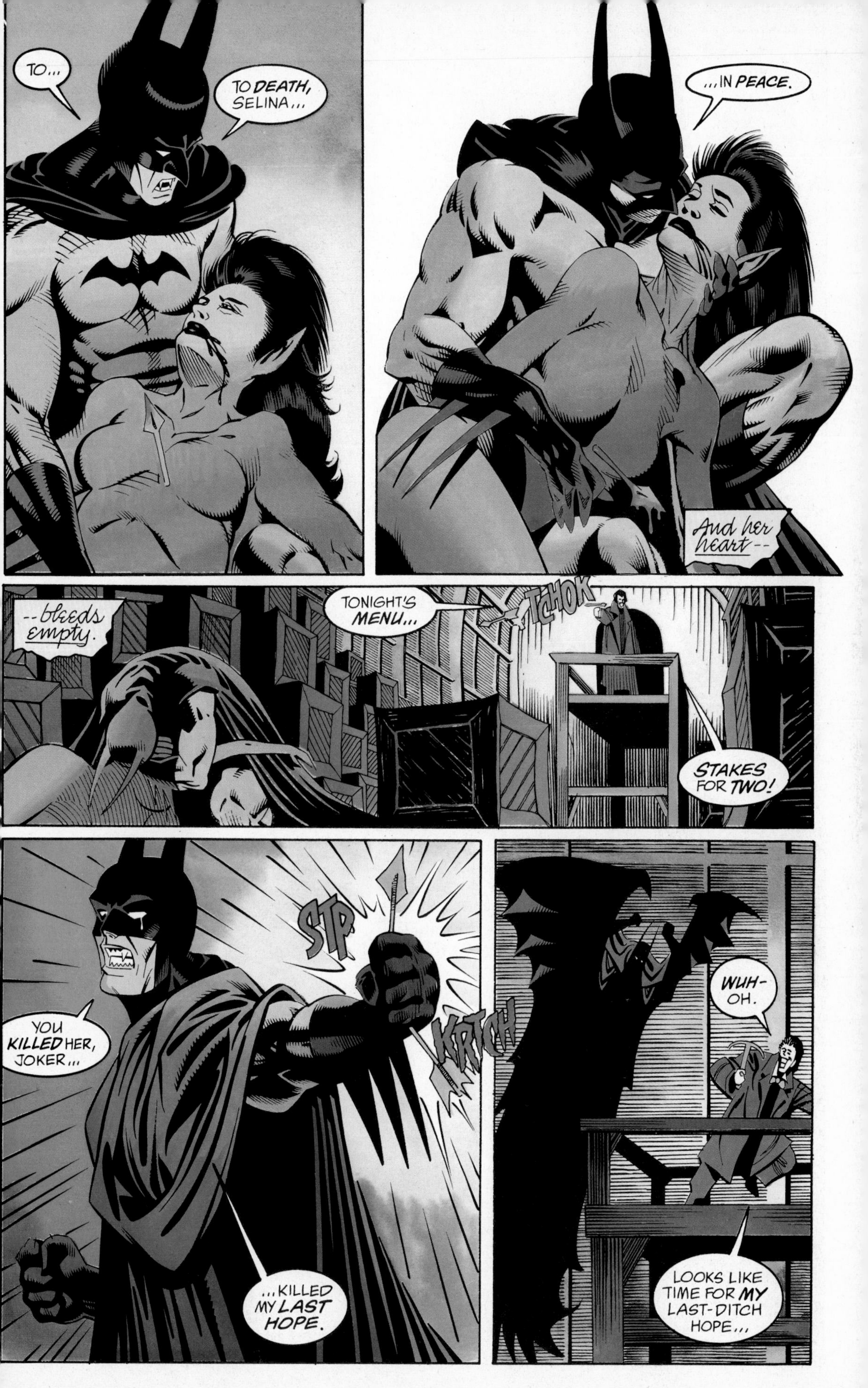
TO...
TO DEATH, SELINA...
...IN PEACE.
And her heart--
--bleeds empty.
TONIGHT'S MENU...
TCHOK
STAKES FOR TWO!
STP
YOU KILLED HER, JOKER...
KRTCH
...KILLED MY LAST HOPE.
WUH-OH.
LOOKS LIKE TIME FOR MY LAST-DITCH HOPE...

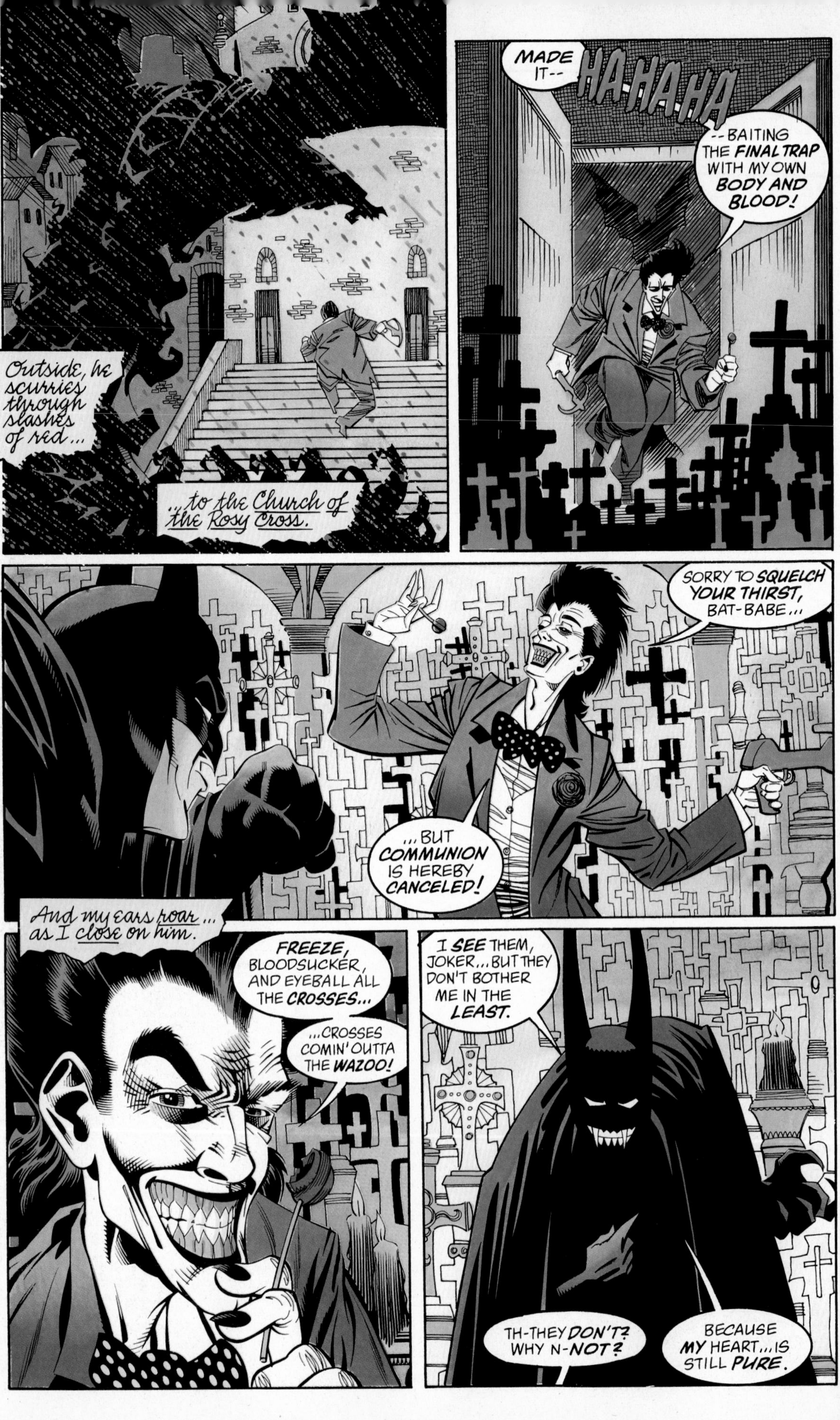
Outside, he scurries through slashes of red...
...to the Church of the Rosy Cross.
MADE IT--
HAHAHA
--BAITING THE FINAL TRAP WITH MY OWN BODY AND BLOOD!
SORRY TO SQUELCH YOUR THIRST, BAT-BABE...
...BUT COMMUNION IS HEREBY CANCELED!
And my ears roar... as I close on him.
FREEZE, BLOODSUCKER, AND EYEBALL ALL THE CROSSES...
...CROSSES COMIN' OUTTA THE WAZOO!
I SEE THEM, JOKER... BUT THEY DON'T BOTHER ME IN THE LEAST.
TH-THEY DON'T? WHY N-NOT?
BECAUSE MY HEART... IS STILL PURE.

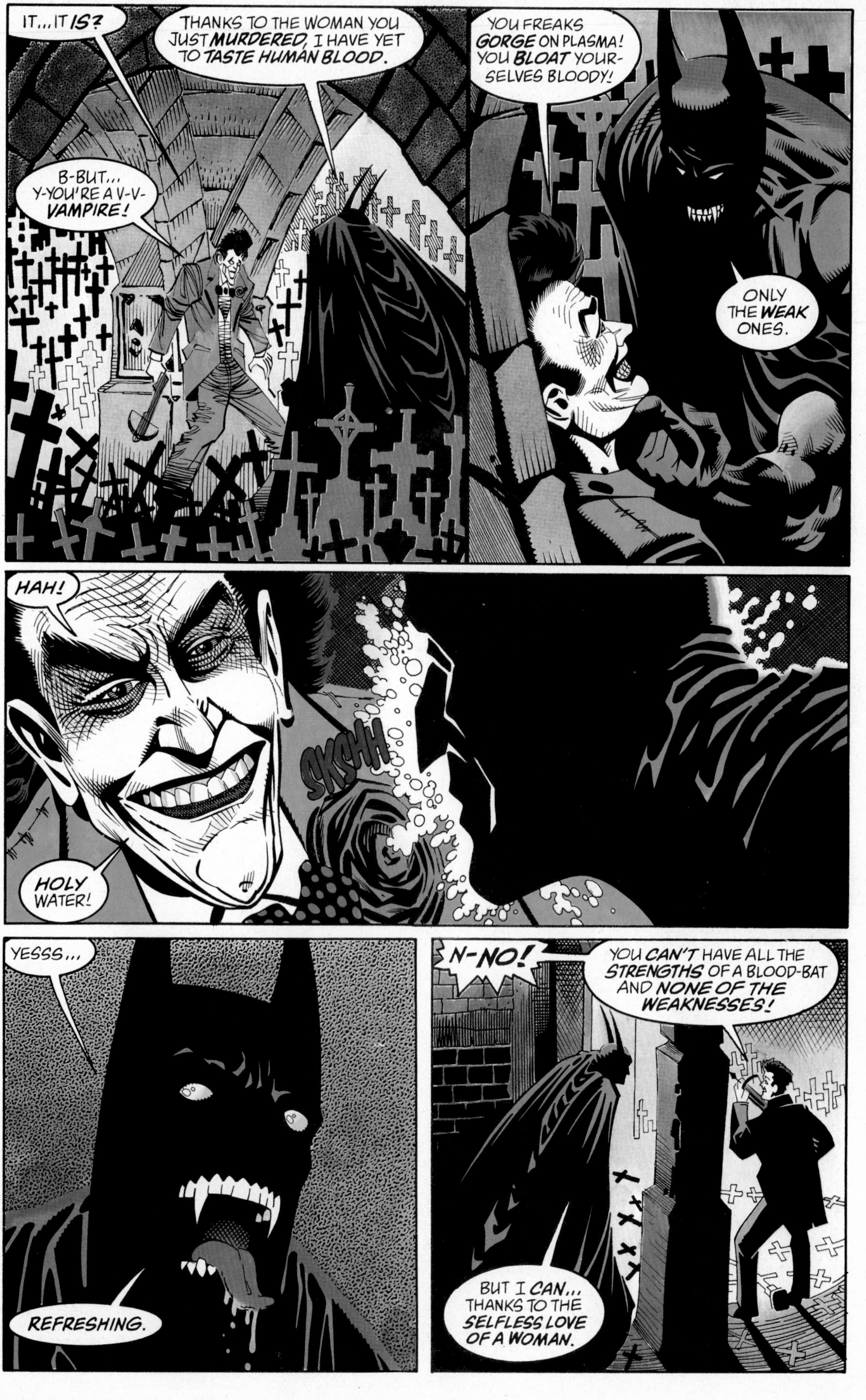
IT... IT IS?
THANKS TO THE WOMAN YOU JUST MURDERED, I HAVE YET TO TASTE HUMAN BLOOD.
B-BUT... Y-YOU'RE A V-V-VAMPIRE!
YOU FREAKS GORGE ON PLASMA! YOU BLOAT YOURSELVES BLOODY!
ONLY THE WEAK ONES.
HAH!
SKSHH
HOLY WATER!
YESSS...
REFRESHING.
N-NO!
YOU CAN'T HAVE ALL THE STRENGTHS OF A BLOOD-BAT AND NONE OF THE WEAKNESSES!
BUT I CAN... THANKS TO THE SELFLESS LOVE OF A WOMAN.

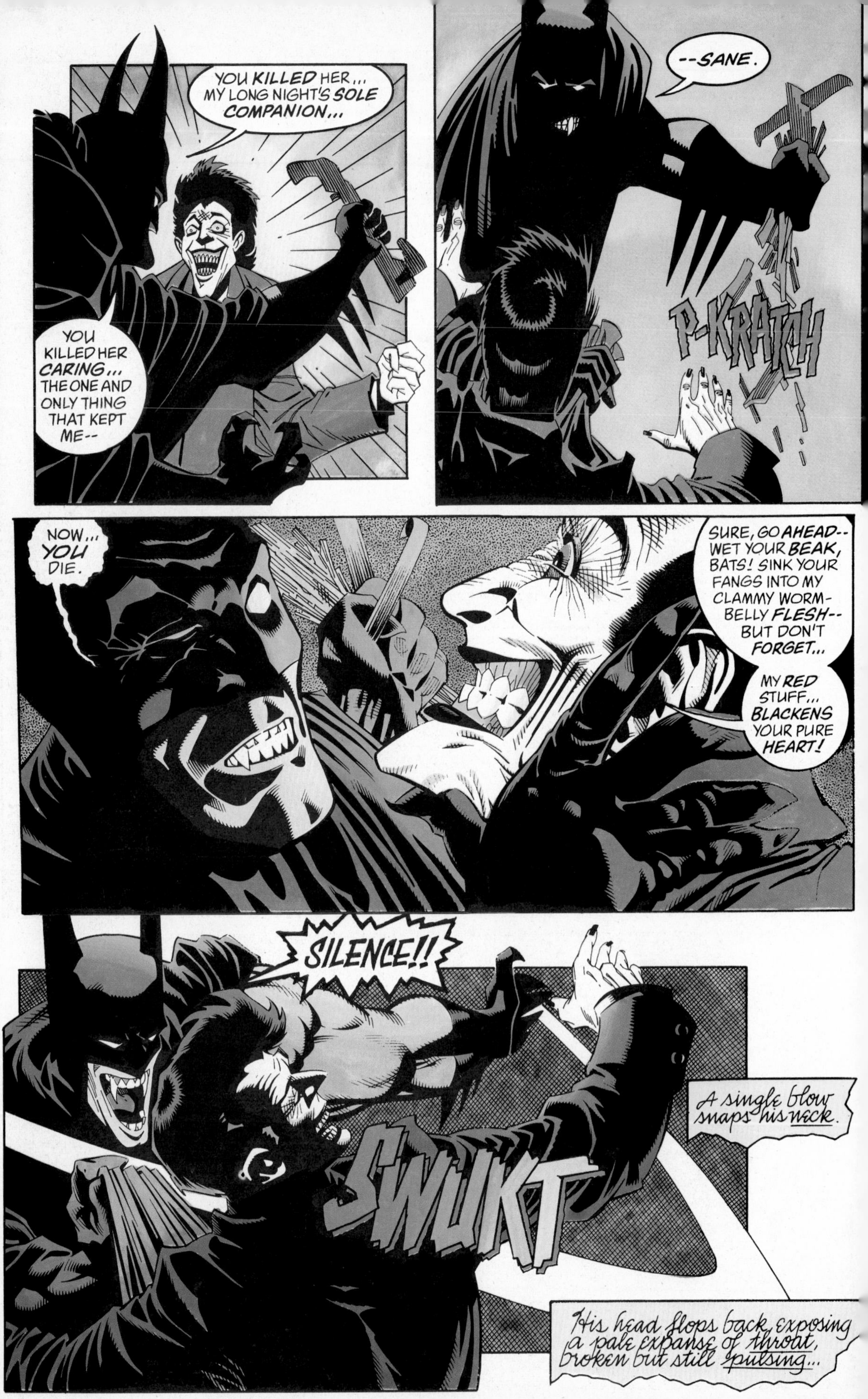
YOU KILLED HER... MY LONG NIGHT'S SOLE COMPANION...
YOU KILLED HER CARING... THE ONE AND ONLY THING THAT KEPT ME--
--SANE.
P-KRATCH
NOW... YOU DIE.
SURE, GO AHEAD-- WET YOUR BEAK, BATS! SINK YOUR FANGS INTO MY CLAMMY WORM-BELLY FLESH-- BUT DON'T FORGET...
MY RED STUFF... BLACKENS YOUR PURE HEART!
SILENCE!!
A single blow snaps his neck.
SWUKT
His head flops back, exposing a pale expanse of throat, broken but still pulsing...

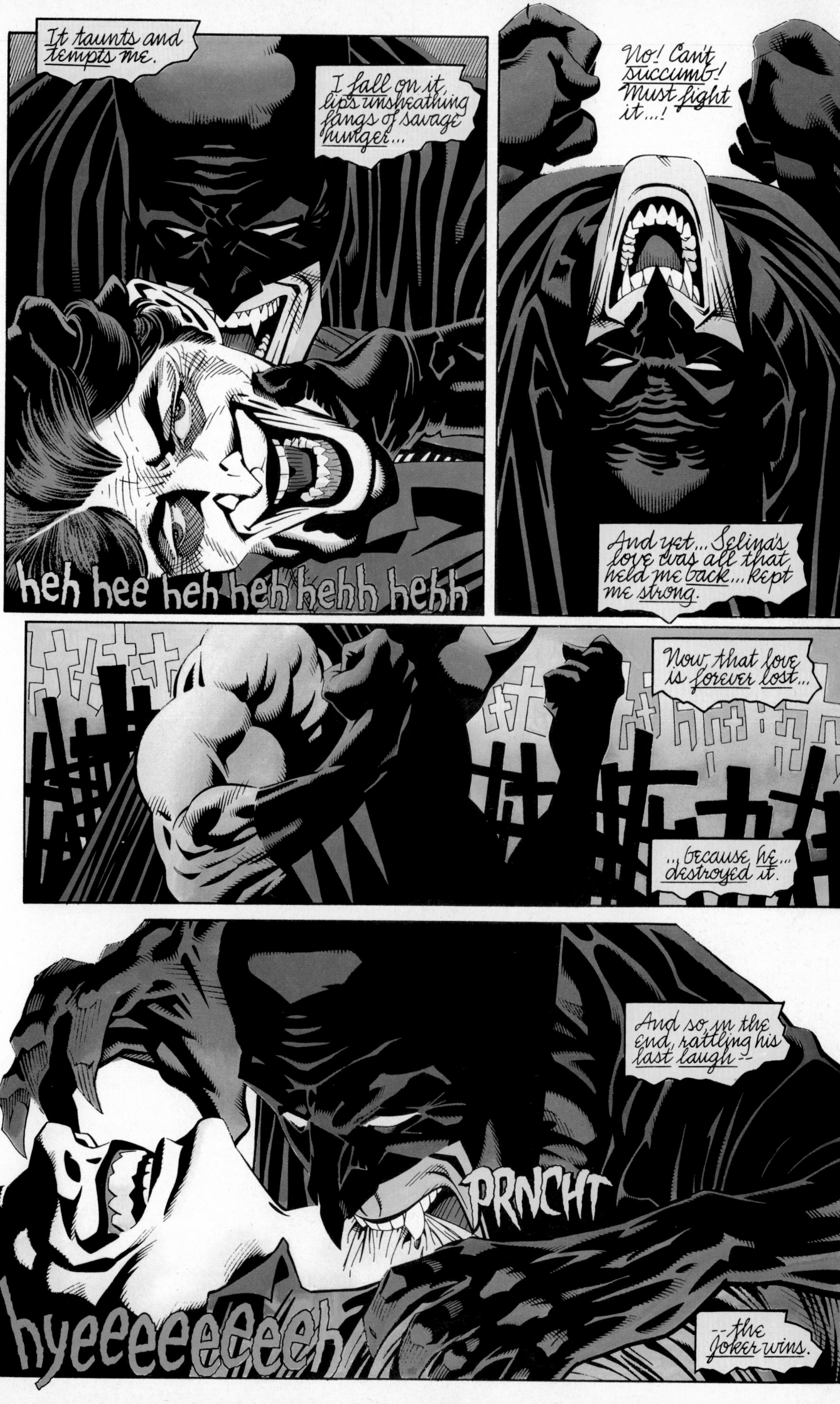
It taunts and tempts me.
I fall on it, lips unsheathing fangs of savage hunger...
heh hee heh heh hehh hehh
No! Can't succumb! Must fight it...!
And yet... Selina's love was all that held me back... kept me strong.
Now, that love is forever lost...
...because he... destroyed it.
And so, in the end, rattling his last laugh--
PRNCHT
hyeeeeeeeeeh
--the Joker wins.

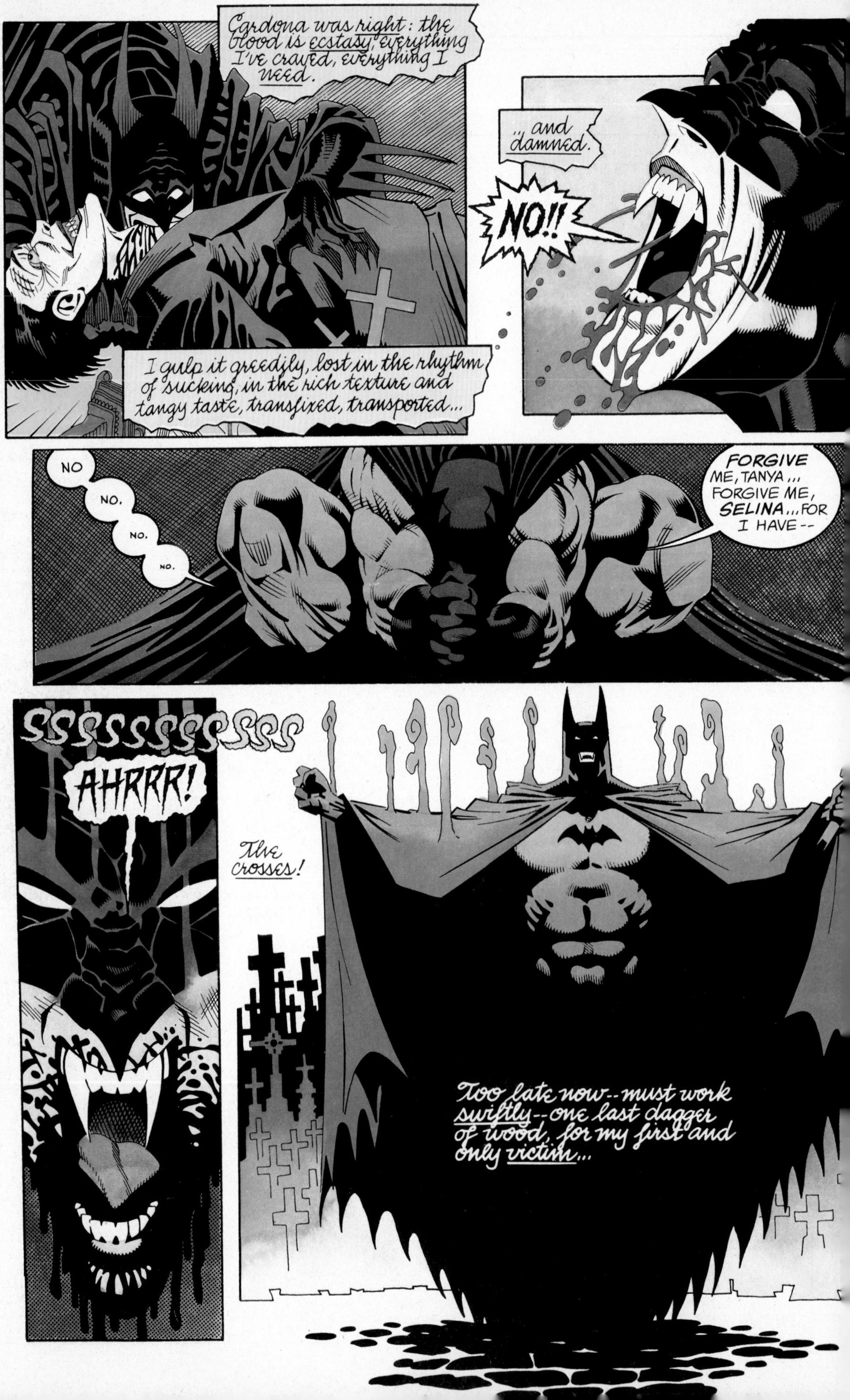
Cardona was right: the blood is ecstasy, everything I've craved, everything I need.
I gulp it greedily, lost in the rhythm of sucking, in the rich texture and tangy taste, transfixed, transported...
...and damned.
NO!!
NO
NO.
NO.
NO.
FORGIVE ME, TANYA... FORGIVE ME, SELINA... FOR I HAVE--
SSSSSSSSSSSS
AHRRR!
The crosses!
Too late now--must work swiftly--one last dagger of wood, for my first and only victim...

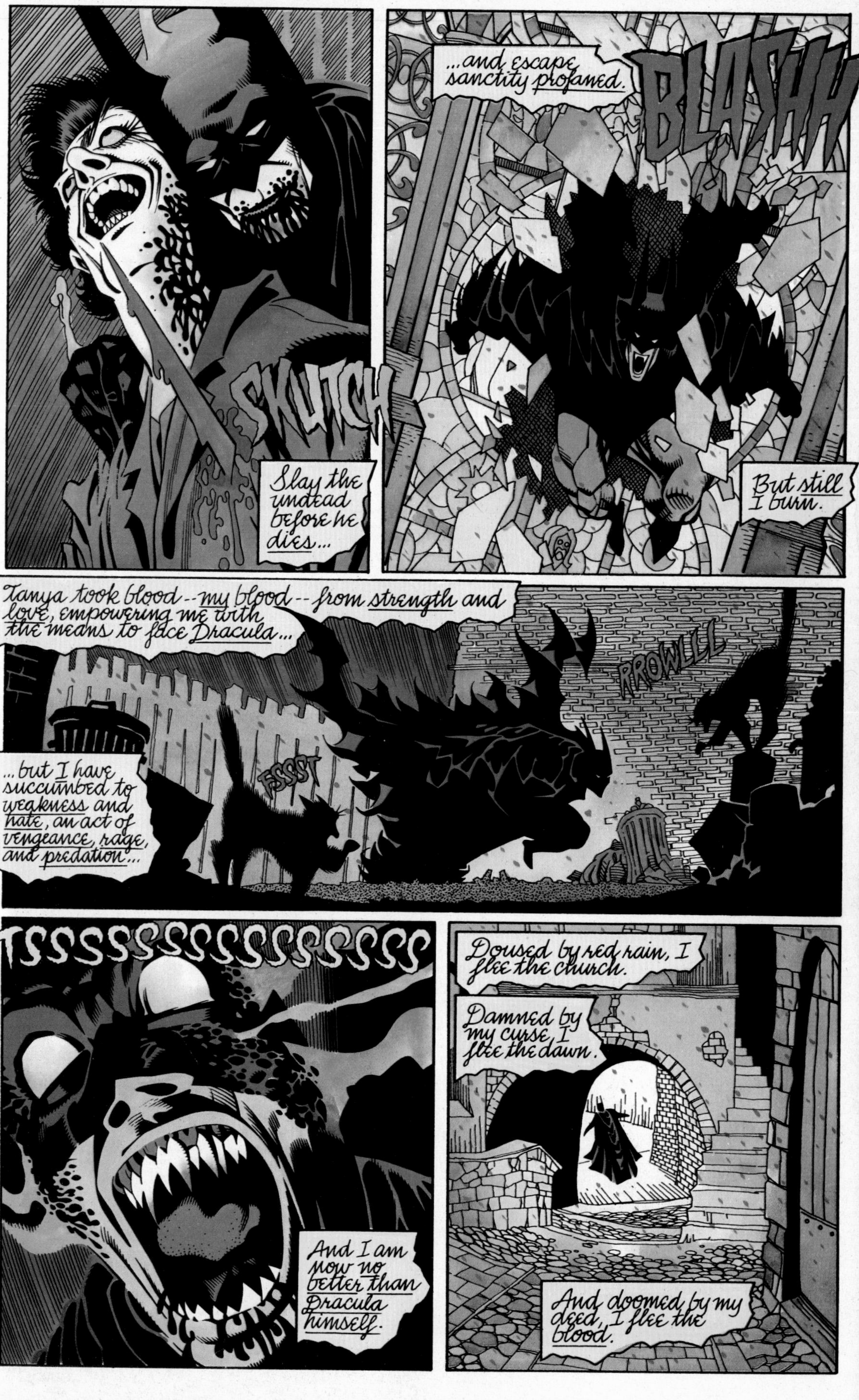
SKUTCH
Slay the undead before he dies...
...and escape sanctity profaned.
BLASHH
But still I burn.
Tanya took blood--my blood--from strength and love, empowering me with the means to face Dracula...
RROWLLL
FSSST
...but I have succumbed to weakness and hate, an act of vengeance, rage, and predation...
TSSSSSSSSSSSSSSSS
And I am now no better than Dracula himself.
Doused by red rain, I flee the church.
Damned by my curse, I flee the dawn.
And doomed by my deed, I flee the blood.

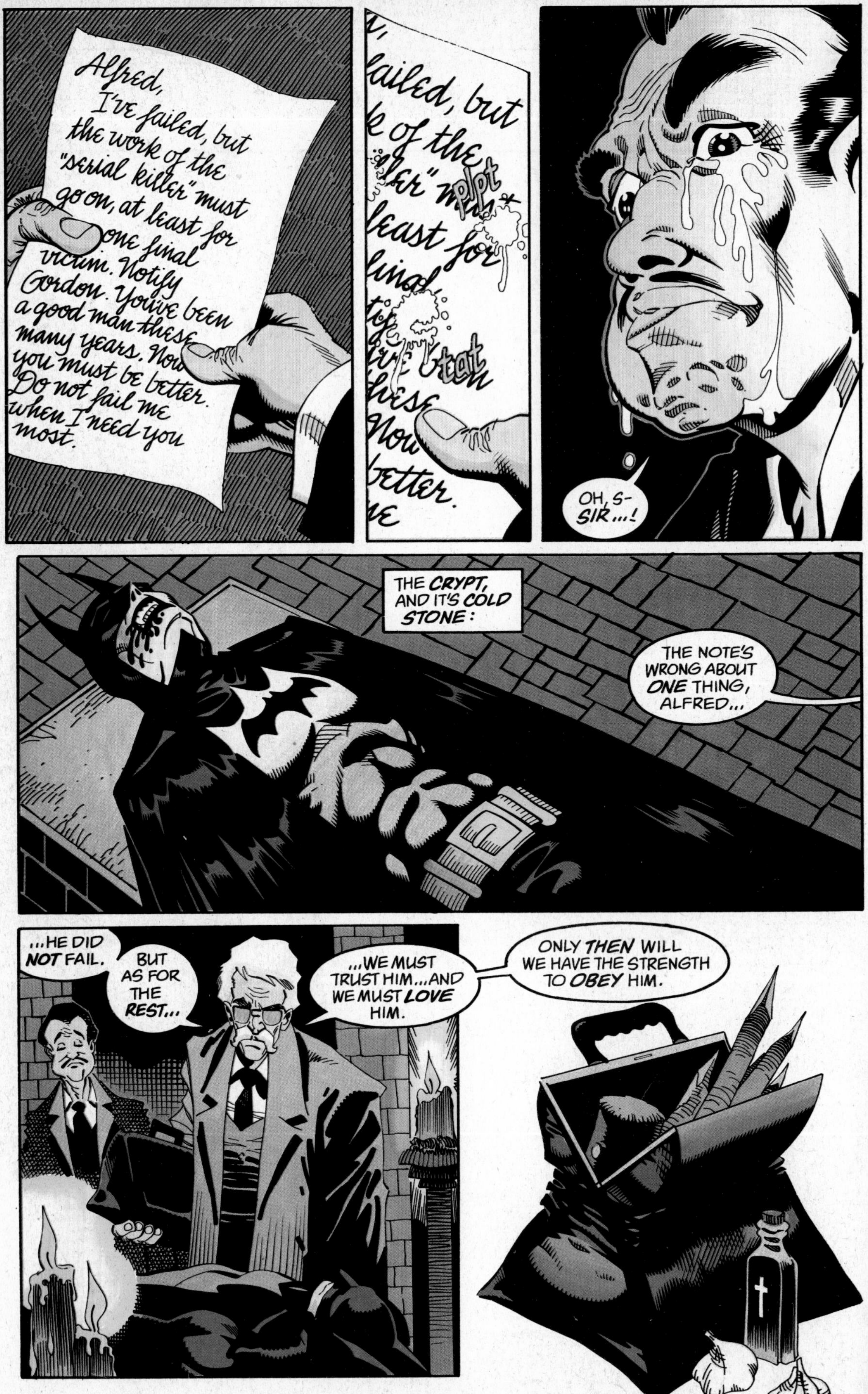
Alfred,
I've failed, but
the work of the
"serial killer" must
go on, at least for
one final
victim. Notify
Gordon. You've been
a good man these
many years. Now
you must be better.
Do not fail me
when I need you
most.
ailed, but
k of the
ller"
plpt
least for
final
tat
these
Now
better.
OH, S-SIR...!
THE CRYPT, AND IT'S COLD STONE:
THE NOTE'S WRONG ABOUT ONE THING, ALFRED...
...HE DID NOT FAIL.
BUT AS FOR THE REST...
...WE MUST TRUST HIM...AND WE MUST LOVE HIM.
ONLY THEN WILL WE HAVE THE STRENGTH TO OBEY HIM.